LEAN *for* MSME

LEAN
for
MSME

A study on the development of the lean practice model for micro, small, and medium-sized enterprises in India's exports since the era of globalization

DR. ANURAG SHARMA

EXCELLER BOOKS®
A GLOBAL PRESS

LEAN for MSME

A study on the development of the lean practice model for micro, small, and medium-sized enterprises in India's exports since the era of globalization

Cover by Exceller Books using resources from Pixabay.com

ISBN: 978-93-48892-72-0
First published in India in 2025 by Exceller Books,
An imprint of GE Group
Address: G1, Dream Apartment, Degree College Road, Belgharia, Kolkata, 700056, India
www.excellerbooks.com

EXCELLER BOOKS®
A GLOBAL PRESS

Acknowledgement

I extend my sincere gratitude to my family for their endless patience and to my colleagues and mentors who shaped my understanding of these concepts. This book is a tribute to all the dedicated professionals who strive for excellence in their daily work.

Table of Contents

Abstract

Rapid globalization and emerging technologies and practices affect the MSME sectors, especially manufacturing units worldwide. Micro, Small, and Medium Enterprises remain in high-risk positions because of competitive market pressure and high expectations from original equipment manufacturers. Hence, MSMEs must function responsively to customer demands and meet expectations for the right quality. Original equipment manufacturers are now compelling their suppliers to continuously increase the rate and implement Lean Manufacturing tools and techniques according to their production volume. This has created new perspectives and pressure on small- and medium-sized enterprises to produce quality products. Many quality concepts and tools are available for improvement, such as Lean Manufacturing, Six Sigma, Lean Six Sigma, etc.

Lean practices are the appropriate management method based on waste management principles while maximizing quality and flexibility. The research's primary goal is to visualize the development of a Lean Practice Model for Micro, Small, and Medium Scale Enterprises in India Exports. The research study also identifies the Critical Success Factors of Lean Manufacturing implementation for small- and medium-sized industries and performance measures through secondary data-based research. The research further articulates and develops the meanings and operational standards of such factors and organizations' performance measures by involving industry owners, operations managers, or employees practicing the Lean Manufacturing technique as the appropriate tool. Finally, the Lean Practice model for lean manufacturing is developed and validated in various small- and medium-scale industries in India. A significant contribution of the developed model is its ability to increase export contribution to India's GDP by implementing Lean tools in MSMEs. It also supports SMEs in standardizing/managing processes, reducing waste at all stages, controlling costs, improving profits, and enhancing customer satisfaction indirectly.

The study's primary goal is to validate and test the credibility of a model proposed by various lean experts to identify Critical Success Factors (CSFs) as foundational components of implementing lean practices within SMEs: leadership, operations, organizational culture, and expertise. This research reviews and discusses CSFs proposed in developing a lean model. Then, methods and concepts associated with lean techniques are implemented. Next, the focal MSME's CSFs (e.g., leadership, management, finance, organizational culture, and skills and expertise) are compared to the Lean model. Finally, it is observed and documented that the focal MSME's lean operational excellence and business processes bring business turnaround and contribute to India's SME exports. This study found that adopting lean practices within an MSME can improve performance if CSFs are considered foundational building blocks and can contribute to India's exports.

The study has been split into seven chapters. The Introduction chapter presents the research's structure and layout, reflecting the flow of the overall research process. The second chapter examines Lean and MSMEs in the Indian context. The same chapter focuses on the SAP-LAP model, which permits the concise presentation of the present situation of manufacturing MSMEs, identification of gaps in lean adoption, and suggestions for improvement in the operational framework.

The third chapter focuses on the growth and performance evaluation of India's MSMEs, the identification of lean tools and practices, and lean measurement systems and models. The fourth chapter, the core chapter of our study, concentrates on developing an integrated lean model and its practices in various MSMEs in India. The fifth chapter analyses the export performance of the small- and medium-sized industry sector vis-à-vis the total export from India. It also addresses the export trend of principal commodities from the small-scale industry sector and the total exports of these commodities from India. The penultimate chapter attempts to identify the problems and prospects of MSME exports from India and provides measures to promote exports from this sector. The final chapter summarizes the study with a SWOT analysis and presents the conclusion.

Chapter I | Introduction

India's 'Make in India' initiative has positioned the country as a significant player in global manufacturing. Many Indian companies seek to adopt lean management principles to attain long-term strategic advantages. Consequently, there is a growing need for a comprehensive lean evaluation system specifically tailored for Indian Micro, Small, and Medium-sized Enterprises (MSMEs) to assess their current lean status and identify potential enhancements for gaining substantial strategic benefits.

Lean is an efficient manufacturing concept that evolved from the Toyota Production System in the 20th century. It is built on the principle of defining value from the customer's perspective and continuously improving how value is supplied by removing all inefficient resource use that does not add up to the value chain.

Since its inception in 1990, it has been successfully implemented in manufacturing and mainly service organizations worldwide. It has become a panacea for all manufacturing services and brought about a dramatic improvement in excellence. However, no missions succeeded primarily because of the non-judicious use of different lean practices and the absence of a proper measurement system.

There are different interpretations of the word 'Lean' that offer the following definition:

Focusing on customers' values, aligning the purpose of essential and support processes around providing these customer values; focusing on ensuring the entire organization is dedicated to supporting process optimization by eliminating waste, improving foundational elements like quality capabilities, empowering individuals and teams, and fostering inter-organizational relationships; and additionally, promoting a system-wide mindset geared towards continual improvement.

Several middle and senior-level executives of global companies are familiar with lean concepts, yet many owners and operators of MSMEs lack proper clarity of the term (Asltonen & Ikavalko, 2002). Even if some people are well aware of the terminology and the concepts, they are not knowledgeable about implementing a lean methodology. Many executives focus only on the methods without considering the existing environment and organizational norms.

According to recent research, process transformation was feasible in the Finnish MSME environment. The same was achieved using lean practices of continuous improvement (CI) and reducing process waste in the flow. However, most small and medium-sized enterprises (SMEs) failed miserably in their process transformation because of the inadequate lean deployment methodology. Findings suggested that having an adequate customized lean deployment methodology could make SMEs more rational in their lean implementation journey, and the chances of failure could be minimized. Early identification of potential causes could make an enterprise more aware of its competencies and weaknesses. A comprehensive process-focused lean implementation model was also suggested. According to the model, the lean implementation program should start with the strategic analysis of market-driven customer requirements and then form a cross-functional team, make a judicious selection of lean tools, perform value stream mapping, and other related steps.

Indian SMEs are the backbone of the Indian economy, employing millions of people. However, to maintain their competitive edge, they need to focus on lean performance. A robust lean performance measurement system could provide crucial insights into their weaknesses in lean tool selection and subsequent implementation. By taking suitable corrective measures, these SMEs can enhance their leanness and gain sustainable strategic advantages over their competitors.

The ultimate goal of the research work is to validate and test the credibility of a model proposed by various lean experts to identify critical success factors (CSFs) as foundational components of implementing lean practices within SMEs: leadership, operations, organizational culture, and expertise. This research reviews and discusses CSFs proposed in developing a lean model. Then, practices and concepts associated with lean techniques are implemented. Next, the focal MSMEs and CSFs (e.g., leadership, management, finance, organizational culture, skills, and expertise) are compared to the lean model. Finally, it is observed and documented that the focal MSME's lean operational excellence and business processes bring business turnaround and contribute to India's SME export. This study found that adopting lean practices within an MSME can improve if CSFs are foundational building blocks and contribute to India's exports.

1.1. Importance of Study

Small and medium-sized enterprises are all important for the Indian economy. Manufacturing played a significant role over the period of time and competence in these enterprises. Small as well as medium-sized enterprises may also become workable in their operational activities in comparison with large enterprises. However, end users are more focused on costs as a result of market globalization. Additionally, economies of scale frequently help big organizations. In addition, large companies often benefit from economies of scale. SMEs must therefore improve their operations in order to maintain their competitiveness continuously.

Applying the lean mindset is a practical and well-designed strategy to turn around the business and encourage continuous improvement. Lean covers a bundle of management techniques and a way of thinking that are completely focused on increasing output. These techniques include Just-in-Time (JIT), continuous flow and improvement, production, and operational flow optimization.

Lean has become a trendy topic in academic research in recent years. Many facts and figures of lean have been discussed in the review literature. For example, the lean supply chain management (SCM) literature was reviewed. However, as stated, there is still a gap between theory and its practical implications in lean manufacturing. Therefore, going forward with all the evidence, more empirical research work is still required. Empirical lean research has been popular in Western countries, especially in countries like the United States (US) and United Kingdom-based companies, particularly in the automotive, Information Technology and Communication, and electronics (ICTE) industries. However, empirical research focusing on lean manufacturing in Indian small and medium-sized enterprises is currently inadequate and an untouched area, particularly in small service sector segments, which is a key motivation for this study. Thus, there is huge potential for these MSMEs to gain benefits through proper planning and execution of lean techniques, which sometimes becomes necessary to analyse by diving deep into practical projects.

This study centres on Indian MSMEs and aims to elaborate the analysis of the development projects for the case companies that used the lean philosophy to accelerate production and increase export performance.

1.1.1. Lean and Toyota's Production System

Toyota's production system (TPS) is the foundation of the lean production system. Massachusetts Institute of Technology (MIT) coined the term lean in 1990 to redefine the Toyota production system as a lean manufacturing system. Lean is the strategy to reduce cost while continuously improving the quality of all products and services delivered, enhancing customer satisfaction.

Leanness gives the measures of lean and has been defined in several ways by researchers worldwide. The impacts of various lean tools and practices used on the lean performance of organizations were termed leanness. Leanness is a term used to describe the degree of commitment to lean manufacturing. Leanness extends beyond lean tools and techniques to almost every aspect of an organization's strategy, including process flow design, maintenance, quality, and safety. The level of perfection in value stream mapping (VSM) is mentioned as leanness. Leanness is the level at which waste is eliminated, ongoing improvements are made, and zero defects are produced. Leanness is the degree to which waste is eliminated due to redundant processes, inefficient operations, and excessive inventory accumulation.

1.1.2. SMEs and International Trade

The importance of international trade in economic development is well acknowledged. Many countries in economic history have success stories of being relatively undeveloped but becoming developed through international trade. Trade provides various static and dynamic benefits, hence increasing growth capability.

The overall economic and social structure must be restructured as a part of the composite process of economic development. Though it is a very composite process influenced by economic and various non-economic factors, these factors include capital stock, labour skills, technology, capital output ratio, agricultural surpluses, foreign trade, etc. Largely, it all determines the place and pattern of the economic development process of a nation. The foreign trade of various goods and services and assets has been termed a unique factor for capital growth and development and one of the potent linkages between the world's various economies.

In addition to promoting economic growth, export promotion tactics provide economies with a bundle of advantages, including accelerated plant capacity utilization, comparative advantage specialisation, increased efficiency, economies of scale, goods market expansion, implications of incentives for technological advancement, upgraded labour training, and internally competitive management. Also, export growth for MSMEs is a crucial step in the economic development process, and its failure can only be acceptable as a development risk.

The performance of small and medium-sized industries in India has been promising regarding export potential. Nevertheless, similar to other developing countries in Asia mentioned earlier, the complete transformation of this sector will hinge on its capacity to transition to advanced and complex technological product and process lines.

We all know that until the economic liberalisation, the Indian economy was virtually isolated on the global platform. The focus was on national manufacturing and protecting domestic industries from both internal and external competitiveness. High tariff barriers, quantitative import limitations, and an internal authorisation and control mechanism provided the means to discourage foreign competition. In this regard, the manufacturing sector retreated inwards and accorded export promotion a lower priority. Until 1991, the Government of India's trade policy was self-centred. A lack of competitiveness emerged from a highly varied industrial structure, which resulted in inadequate attention to research and development, reduction in costs, and improvement of merchandise and technological procedures. It caused India's share in world trade to go down from 2 percent at independence to roughly 0.62 percent in 1991.

Since 1971-72, the SSI sector has expanded at a remarkable rate, and its proportion of the country's exports has grown from 9.6 percent in 1971-72 to 26.51 percent in 1981-82 and 31.52 percent in 1991-92.

Additionally, it was 30.51 percent in 2018-19 and 30.01 percent in 2019-20. MSME manufacturing accounted for 36.91 percent of India's total manufacturing gross value-added output in the years 2018-19 and 2019-20. The Directorate General of Commercial Intelligence and Statistics (DGCIS) said that in 2019-20 and 2020-21, the export share of particular MSME-related procedures to all Indian exports was 49.82 percent and 49.51 percent, respectively. Despite the various value contributions of the SSI sector, the fact that our share of global trade remained stagnant at 0.61 to 0.80 percent for almost 20 years implies that, had the small industries sector not provided significantly favourable conditions, our share may have further gone down to 0.3 or 0.4 percent of global trade.

However, the MSME sector over the period of time has grown to be a significant one and helped India gain a 2.1 percent share in global trade in 2016-17. Exports have been growing regularly since 2016-17 for almost three years, and total exports reached a new height of more than half a trillion dollars for the very first time in 2018-19. Since 2010-11, the MSME sector has contributed consistently to India's growth and has emerged as a vibrant partner by consistently positioning the overall industry segment and contributing to GDP growth.

Post-liberalisation, the small-scale industry environment changed drastically. The situation enjoyed was exceedingly reduced through delicensing, reduction and reconsideration in government excise and customs duty rates, presentation of various items on the OGL list, and by making creditworthiness the criterion for credit disbursement. Small-scale industries faced high-level competition from a number of foreign firms. On the other hand, the small-scale industry was expected to act as an engine of growth for the national economy. In other words, by using its flexible, easily transferable, and innovative nature, the SSI is expected to work as a linkage and subcontracting or export-oriented industry.

Against this background, it was observed that the export performance of MSME sectors vis-à-vis India's total exports has been reduced. Moreover, we have tried to analyse the implementation of various lean tools and techniques, and this will help an MSME improve overall quality, eliminate waste, reduce total costs, and shorten the time it takes to complete an operation from start to end. Various qualitative, quantitative, and monetary benefits are likely to be realised through

Lean Tools. Thus, this will help accelerate the current performance and contributions to exports in the present economic circumstances. Further, I have suggested distinguished measures for promoting small-scale industry exports with policy implications.

1.2. Relevance of Study

In today's dynamic manufacturing environment, companies frequently find themselves navigating their customers' constantly changing needs and choices. Embracing lean practices not only aims to give employees more autonomy but also seeks to elevate their job satisfaction and foster a greater sense of fulfillment, ultimately instilling a strong sense of pride in their work. It ensures that manufacturing processes become leaner and fitter and eliminates all kinds of waste that do not add any value to the product. In today's global market, it has become essential for Indian manufacturing industries to embrace a lean manufacturing system to remain competitive and retain their market share. With lean practices, Indian industries endeavour to empower workers, increase job satisfaction, and facilitate a sense of accomplishment, creating pride in work. This research work presents a deep study of lean manufacturing adopted and benefited by MSMEs in terms of increasing their contribution margin to India's GDP.

1.3. Statement of Problems

Today, MSMEs are flourishing in a well-organised, cluster-based manner. However, globalisation and new technologies significantly impact the manufacturing industry in the present era. Due to liberalisation and globalisation, Indian MSMEs are facing tremendous challenges. Imports and MNCs are becoming significant threats to Indian industries. For many sectors abroad, lean thinking is a way of life as it eliminates waste and improves the efficiency of an organisation. However, in India, lean implementation is still in its early stages. Lean manufacturing has yet to receive due attention in MSMEs globally. Thus, this research work deals with identifying the critical issues in the implementation of lean in Indian MSMEs, and attempts have been made to provide realistic solutions to overcome significant barriers identified for the effective execution of lean.

1.4. Objectives of the Study

The primary goal of this study is to examine the development of the lean practice model and its effectiveness in the export growth of MSMEs since the globalisation era (mainly the period 2005–2020) to determine the factors influencing the sector's export performance. Under the scope of this broad objective, the study will aim to achieve the following specific objectives:

- To analyse how the lean practice model has developed and how well it has performed for the MSME sector's export performance since the globalisation era (2005–2020) in relation to India's overall export output.
- To identify the main issues confronting MSME exports.
- To analyse the capability of Indian MSMEs within the global value chain and target new export milestones.
- To suggest measures to realise the full export potential of the MSME sector in the long run.

1.5. Data Base and Methodology

The research study is based on primary and secondary data sources covering mainly the period 2005–06 to 2019–20, which were acquired from the following sources:

- Survey, questionnaires, and personal interviews – used to collect information.
- SIDBI (Small Industries Development Bank of India) Report on Micro, Small and Medium Enterprises, 2019–20, SIDBI, Lucknow.
- Economic Survey, 2019–20, Department of Commerce (The Commerce Ministry), Govt. of India, New Delhi.
- Indian Brand Equity Foundation (IBEF), MSME Indian Economy.
- DCMSME (Development Commissioner, Ministry of Micro, Small and Medium Enterprises): Lean Evaluation Performance of Indian SMEs.
- http://www.dcmsme.gov.in/publications

Proper acknowledgment has been given where it is due.

For various analyses, the time period is restricted from 2005–06 to 2019–20. Years before 2005 were not taken into account due to the nonexistence or incomplete availability of data regarding the implementation of lean methodology and its impact on total exports of some key manufactured commodities.

The basic variables considered in the research work are the selection of lean tools, exports of the commodity, production system, firms' employment, and the number of units measured. The applied methodology will be a simple lean analytical approach to calculate percentages, arithmetic mean, simple rate of growth, and compound rate of growth.

In the case of MSMEs, the compound annual growth rates (CAGR) will be calculated for production, employment, exports, and the number of units during the study period. This rate will be computed for total exports from India and exports of various principal commodities, both from MSMEs and the total exports of these items from India.

Simple growth rate indicates the progress or otherwise on a year-to-year basis. The following formula is used to determine the simple growth rate:

$SGR = (Y_t) - (Y_{t-1}) / (Y_{t-1}) *100$

Where,

SGR – Simple Growth Rate

Y_t – Base Year Value

Y_{t-1} – Previous Year Value

CAGR is a figure that represents the yearly growth rate of an investment over a specified time frame. It provides a single, smooth rate at which an investment with an initial value grows annually to reach its current value. The compounded growth rate is particularly useful for comparing the growth of distinguished investments over time.

$CAGR = [(X_t / X_0)^{1/t} - 1]*100$

Where,

CAGR – Compound Annual Growth Rate

X_0 – Base Year Value

X_t – Value of the Final Year

t – Time frame or the number of years considered in the calculation

1.6. Review of Literature

1.6.1. Overview

Reviewing the existing literature provides an initial starting point in defining lean manufacturing practices adopted by various industries. It also helps us highlight the confusion in the conceptual success factors and the operational issues around lean practice, and gather a set of lean operational measures that can be used to represent the performance of any organization.

In conducting the review process, we began with the earliest publications on Japanese manufacturing/production systems, ending with the most recent publications on lean practice. We observed that, in general, the early Japanese books were more precise in defining Lean and identifying its underlying components (Monden, 1983) than the research articles, because the latter focused on defining and describing specific elements of the system rather than the whole. Small and medium enterprises provide the majority of production to the original equipment manufacturer (OEM) and the same amplifications in the other sectors. Therefore, business scenarios and challenges for OEMs oppress them. OEMs are now forcing their suppliers to continuously improve product quality and implement lean methods and tools. This has created new perspectives and pressure for production in small and medium-sized enterprises. Many quality concepts and tools are available for quality improvements, such as lean manufacturing, Six Sigma, Lean Six Sigma, etc.

In the 1980s, the auto industry adopted the lean management philosophy as an operational step. After effectively implementing the lean methodology, Toyota has surpassed auto giants General Motors, Ford Motors, and Chrysler as the number one automaker. Now, to achieve the same benefits as Toyota, the lean production approach has begun to acquire acceptance worldwide in a wide range of industries, including services. It has been observed that a lean manufacturing methodology is more suited to discrete manufacturing than continuous manufacturing in the process industry. However, evidence shows that a lean manufacturing system has been followed successfully in process industries such as chemicals and pharmaceuticals.

There are several historical substantiations of export-oriented growth in different countries worldwide. Chen (1986) asserts that "the experiences of Japan, Hong Kong, South Korea, Singapore, and Taiwan suggest that the successful export growth requires a very strong and viable small industrial sector. Due to labour-intensive products, high fluctuations in demand due to global economic fluctuations and demand-driven output growth, the small industries can play a vital role in the early stages of manufacturing export growth. Small industries have the advantage of low running costs and the ability to react swiftly in changing conditions. In substitute of mass-produced things, there is a consistently growing international leaning for high-quality personalised items that are typically labour-intensive, a trend that bodes well for the future of small-scale industries. Such items necessitate flexibility, which frequently favours the smaller company."

According to Beng (1988), "Establishing a reliable support network has been pivotal in attracting foreign investment in high technology to Singapore. This has removed the necessity for international companies to hire external subcontractors or bring in foreign workers, aligning with the long-term goals of government policy. In various countries such as Hong Kong, Japan, Singapore, and Taiwan, subcontracting with small-scale producers has empowered the export sector to maintain competitive costs and flexibility. Furthermore, the absorptive capacity of small firms significantly contributes to technology transfer. For instance, in Singapore, skilled personnel trained by multinational corporations often transition to smaller local firms or establish their own businesses, serving as a key channel for technology dissemination and growth."

In their study, Hackman and Wageman (1995) focus on total quality management, which is made up of empirical, conceptual, and practical issues. Total quality management (TQM) is "pro-learning, with a vengeance." The published work on lean should place a greater focus on the learning elements. The literature on lean focuses primarily on instrumental techniques for increasing system output and is typically weaker on the human lean behaviour side. Since the objective is continuous improvement (CI), learning of some kind must happen, but who is learning is a question. While lean is majorly focused on standardised work and group learning, TQM is more focused on adding creativity and one's initiatives for turning around the process output.

Adler (1995) and Bano and Jordan (1999) have highlighted that companies that implement lean practices tend to increase leanness, while Reinhart et al. (1997) have similarly suggested that companies that adopt lean end up with excessive lean, which increases efficiency but reduces employee satisfaction. However, Graham (1995) and Milkman (1997) stated that companies adopting lean pay more for their employees, while Vidal (2007) stated that lean leads to increased workload and responsibility falling on the workers, so they tend to believe all these things will improve job satisfaction among the employees.

Kettinger and Grover (1995) quote that a significant change in the process requires the following success factors: strategic investment; managers acting as leaders in defining and communicating the change vision; the desire to learn; preparation for culture; retained relationships network; knowledge exchange; prescribed processes and change management methods. Failures lie mainly in implementing Lean with ageing and then work duty and lack of leadership involved in this research on the site. Grove et al. (2010) identified the obstacles they face during a lean implementation in a healthcare environment. (Mefford, 2009) identified the following four essential components for successful implementation of lean: belief that the new programme will work; commitment to the implementation by managers; participation of the entire organisation – employees, resources; and patience and a long-term vision for the results. According to Pedersen and Huniche (2011), the following factors are important for the implementation: goals and values; complexity and importance; balance of power; and the resources and capacity.

Ahlstrom (1998), in his study, aims to contribute to 'Sequences in implementing lean production.' When a company is considering improving its manufacturing performance, a key decision is whether to pursue improvement initiatives simultaneously or one after the other. This research study examines the feasibility of implementing sequences of manufacturing improvement initiatives and identifies potential sequences. Based on a two-and-a-half-year involvement in implementing lean production at a specific company, the author's research categorises lean production principles into four groups based on when management invests in these principles. The study's findings suggest that there are specific sequences for implementing lean production principles. Furthermore, the study emphasises the importance of management in allocating resources and effort simultaneously to principles.

Pohekar and Ramachandran (2004) analysed the applicability of multi-criteria decision-making methods in the '90s published articles related to renewable energy planning, energy resource allocation, building energy management, transportation energy systems, project planning, and electric utility planning. A primary strength of the Analytic Hierarchy Process is the ability to take into account subjective opinions of decision-makers. This feature has made it especially attractive for combining with other methodologies usually developed to cope with objective data.

Antonio and Ferguson (2004) identified ten key components of success for the company's learning management system, i.e. leadership commitment and commitment from top management, organisational support structures, and cultural exchange; Lean training; customer loyalty and Lean awareness methodology; project management; prioritisation; and project selection. The outcomes of this study show that the most important factors for success are commitment and commitment to the organisation, cultural changes, linking Lean with business strategy, and customer involvement.

Simon and Kleiner (2004) have noted that companies seeking to control costs and increase efficiency through the implementation of Lean must be able to improve the quality of the services provided to customers by increasing quality, reducing operating costs, and increasing profits. A simple goal is to reduce employees and areas that are not showing good results. As a result, employees remain in the organization and fear losing their jobs, which affects their morale and causes harm to the company.

Mefford and Croat (2004) examined the lean thinking process and its development over time. They observed that many critics try to attack the weak points, but what is often overlooked is that Lean has evolved and continues to evolve as a complete management system. Taiichi Ohno developed lean manufacturing at Toyota Motor Company in the 1950s as a new technology based on intellectual and hands-on concepts from the industrial world, as well as Ford's work standards and basic organizational unity. The ability to work together.

Dolan and Hacker (2005) identified several organizational, monetary, and operational factors that influence the implementation of lean practices. Ramesh et al. (2009) showed that by using lean principles and computer simulation, it is possible to improve the production of companies involved in pump manufacturing. Wong (2009) came up with a study of Malaysian energy companies, showing that most companies have largely implemented lean practices.

Altkar (2005) showed that by executing lean methods, companies can achieve a 50 percent increase in energy use and increased efficiency, more than 50 percent reduction in waste, 70 percent reduction in inventory, and 30 percent reduction in production costs. Traditional and labour costs saw a 50 percent reduction in production cycle time. In addition, by implementing lean operations, the flexibility of methods and processes, the quality of production, overall efficiency, working capital, and the ability to respond to emergencies can be increased. Environmental change.

Trev and Anto (2006) have seen the drawbacks of lean implementation and stated that the emphasis on lean increases the risk of work-related major or minor injuries for employees because it can lead to overweight and obesity. Womack (1990) discussed the value of employee job security when implementing lean practices, while Angelis (2011) indicated that job security boosts performance and employee morale.

Vidal (2007) believes that increased responsibility raises stress from higher workloads, mental stress, and depression, which is a burden for employees and not beneficial to them. Kuhlang (2011) indicated in their findings the role of VSM (Value Stream Mapping) and time measurement techniques in reducing time to production and increasing productivity. With an emphasis on lean concepts, the work of Marksberry et al. (2011) showed that lean processes and methods work very well to solve companies' various issues and challenges. Faris et al. (2009) confirmed the effectiveness of kaizen and lean implementation in increasing employees' ability to solve complex problems and boost productivity.

Bakas et al. (2007) in their study observed that small and medium-sized enterprises play a vital role in creating value within the European economy. To remain competitive, SMEs require continuous improvement initiatives. However, it has been seen that small and medium-sized industries are less inclined to adopt lean practices than larger corporations. Further research must identify the critical factors for successful lean implementations in SMEs. A pilot study carried out as part of the European research project, through ERIP (European Regions for Innovative Productivity), focused on Norwegian and Belgian SMEs. The study identified six critical success factors that align with previous research. While the findings confirmed previous research, it was noted that the number of studies in this area is currently limited. The critical success factors (CSF) that have been suggested are:

- Ensuring strong management involvement,
- Developing thorough employee participation,
- Allocating sufficient time for preparing the organization,
- Focusing on creating motivation to complete initiatives, and
- Building competence internally in the organization.

Establish a performance evaluation system, ensure strong leadership and management involvement, allow for thorough employee involvement and sufficient participation, allocate enough time for preparing the organization, make sure there is adequate motivation for completing initiatives, build competence in the internal organization, and ensure a performance evaluation system is established in parallel. The findings outlined in this paper provide essential perspectives for Micro, Small, and Medium Enterprises (MSMEs) aiming to integrate lean manufacturing practices. SMEs frequently encounter challenges due to limited resources and expertise. There is little margin for error with constraints such as tight budgets and time pressure. Adopting a culture of continuous improvement among all employees can yield noteworthy, measurable outcomes both on the production floor and in financial statements. This study draws from the practical experiences of a group of SMEs, providing a valuable opportunity for other companies to learn from the challenges and pitfalls these enterprises encounter.

Baio and Decorvin (2008) indicated that the extent of lean implementation should be measured using a non-logical method, while

Martínez-Jurado and Moyano-Fuentes (2014) believed that the successful implementation of lean must be influenced by various factors such as the company's perception of quality, organizational motivation, current organizational culture to support lean operations, operational support, and operational assistance.

According to Sim and Rogers (2009), the process of real differentiation is problematic. A lack of knowledge, lack of communication and leadership, unclear focus on goals, difficulty in identifying waste problems, and challenges in identifying customers and value from the customer's perspective were noted. Barriers to implementation can be overcome through forward planning, change leadership, effective communication, identification and sharing of best practices, and most importantly, a shared vision.

Kumar et al. (2009) identified the importance of the following success factors when implementing Six Sigma or Lean: organizational commitment and communication, healthy relationships with employees, cultural change, training, client social quality, program choice, quality of business relationships, goodwill with suppliers, purpose, organizational structure, vision and planning, information technology (IT), and innovation.

Rahman (2010) conducted a survey of 187 Thai company managers involved in manufacturing firms and found that micro and small enterprises implemented lean techniques and reduced waste compared to large enterprises. However, large enterprises implemented Lean Just in Time (JIT) and Just Do It (JDI) better than their small and micro counterparts. The research also found a significant impact of JIT and JDI execution by many companies on their performance.

Vinodh & Joy (2011) conducted a research study aiming to analyse lean manufacturing and management practices in different industries and identify the critical factors for their successful implementation. Even though lean manufacturing has been frequently promoted to improve business competitiveness, more empirical evidence is needed in the literature to validate its positive link with organisational performance. By implementing lean manufacturing practices, companies can minimise defects and lower production costs. Empirical data were gathered to gauge the prevalence of lean manufacturing practices across various industries in Tamil Nadu, India. Structural

Equation Modelling (SEM) was then used to construct measurement and structural models. Subsequently, statistical estimates were applied to validate the model. The analysis of the data aided in determining whether to accept or reject the hypotheses formulated based on the structural model. Hence, it was concluded that lean manufacturing practices are correlated and help improve organisational performance among the surveyed industries.

Sahai et al. (2011) noticed that micro and small organisations in India do not have appropriate implementation of smart manufacturing technologies, while Achanga (2006) observed that micro and small enterprises' limited perception of the benefits they can achieve through the execution of lean approaches serves as a major impediment to their adopting lean.

Bakas, Ottar et al. (2011) identified in their study of Norwegian and Belgian SMEs—conducted as part of the European research project EIRP (European Regions for Innovative Productivity)—six proposed critical success factors, which are consistent with previous research:

- Ensuring strong management commitment.
- Developing in-depth employee participation.
- Allocating enough time to prepare the organisation.
- Focusing on creating motivation to complete the initiative.
- Building internal knowledge within the organisation.
- Establishing a performance evaluation system.

Panizzolo (2012) remarked that lean execution among micro and small organisations has been mildly researched. Similarly, Sahay (2011) expressed a comparable opinion. April (2010) opined that MSMEs find it challenging to execute lean principles and practices, among other quality enhancement techniques, due to a lack of monetary and other resources. However, Kumar (2006) pointed out that SMEs can execute lean and Six Sigma concepts to enhance their competitiveness by optimising costs and increasing productivity and quality. Achanga (2006) observed that successful execution of lean methodology by SME businesses depends on organisational culture, talent and skill sets, financial resources, innovative management, and managerial support.

Ghosh (2013) found that a large number of manufacturing organisations in India have adopted lean methodology, focusing on customer satisfaction and needs, setup time reduction, pull process implementation, resolving interdepartmental issues, placing statistical process and control mechanisms, improving supplier performance, and implementing TPM. She also found that the implementation of lean principles and practices resulted in increased output and productivity, reduced operational space, better inventory management, reduced idle time, process lead time, etc.

Kennedy (2013) noticed that traditional manufacturing organisations have only concentrated on implementing lean, even though it is extremely beneficial for business growth in terms of reducing waste and creating value. Lean implementation should also become a top priority for other service industries and modern industries, such as food production.

Marodin and Saurin (2013) focused their study on LP implementation research areas and proposed research opportunities. The growing adoption of lean production (LP) across various industries has led to a significant rise in the volume of literature and diverse perspectives on the subject. This necessitates the organisation of existing knowledge in this area. The review encompassed 102 studies published between 1996 and 2012, categorising them into six key research areas: the structure and scope of LP systems, factors influencing LP implementation, methods for implementing LP systems, LP assessment techniques, outcomes of LP system implementations, and customisation of LP for specific sectors. The findings indicate that the substantial increase in publications on LP implementation has resulted in fragmented and disconnected areas that could benefit from integration.

Marodin and Saurin (2015) stated that the barriers are embedded in a socio-technical system (STS) that shapes their nature, relations, and intensity (i.e., there is a context). The prioritisation and control of the barriers might benefit from understanding their interrelationships. In line with those premises, the proposed framework involves five stages: upon identifying the obstacles, the context's influence on these barriers will be analysed. The relationships between barriers will be explored using interpretive structural modelling (ISM). This analysis will form the basis for prioritising the barriers. Subsequently, a feedback meeting will be held to discuss the results of data collection, which will also provide insights for developing an action plan to control the barriers.

These stages are cyclical, as implementing the action plan will likely modify the context, impacting the barriers.

Adam Taylor (2015) also pointed out that although Six Sigma is successful in controlling processes in which non-value-added activities are reduced and performance is improved, its use raises many issues for both the workforce and the bottom line. Therefore, it is suggested that a company proceed with prudence before implementing lean. As the author pointed out, not all procedures can be executed through lean. According to the report, organisations that implement lean practices streamline their man-hours by reducing, eliminating, and considering only employees who are extraordinary in various activities rather than based on occupation. As a result, Six Sigma has caused staff to be overburdened, which has led to stress and health issues.

Dushyanth Kumar et al. (2016) stated that in most current situations, small and medium-scale industries (SMEs) are struggling in their business due to product variations in the market, economic crises, and competition. To overcome these difficulties, they are announcing voluntary retirement schemes, laying off employees, and in some cases, even shutting down operations. So, instead of increasing the selling price, these industries are considering reducing internal costs to improve product quality. The product depends on the customer, as they determine the market value based on cost and quality. Due to these reasons, this study insists on applying the most effective lean manufacturing principles at different stages of production systems and supply lines. This research aims to incorporate lean manufacturing and supply chain management principles, especially in SMEs, to achieve better product efficiency with reduced cycle time through quantitative analysis, considering the main criteria. Based on the review, some guidelines are also suggested, which offer sound strategies for SCM to ensure sustainable competitive advantage in market share and business performance. Further justification is provided in this work. In this study, the researchers discussed the sustainability and adaptability of lean manufacturing and SCM in small and medium-sized enterprises. Because of their importance in the current market conditions and competition, and for survival, SMEs should focus on improving their existing systems and fulfilling customer needs. One of the approaches that reconsider best management practices for SMEs is leaning toward advanced manufacturing techniques like lean manufacturing principles. The survey has highlighted practical lean practices that must be implemented to achieve success in lean implementation. The systematic implementation of LM principles in supply chain management in SMEs reasonably provides cycle time reduction, quality improvement, and improved customer response.

After reviewing many papers and articles about various lean manufacturing tools and techniques, the authors applied the keywords—critical success factors, performance measures, and lean framework—for inline research tactics. Finally, conceptual critical success factors and the organisation's performance measures for exploring model input and development have been investigated.

1.6.2. Research Gap

The comprehensive review of previous research work has demonstrated that many of the previous studies have focused on the idea of implementing lean practices, showing the elements that make up successful execution along with the result of such implementations that impact, either directly or indirectly, the output of MSMEs in real time. Some lean methodologies have been implemented, nevertheless, and their impacts on productivity have been studied. Similarly, there is an absence of research evidence on how the application of lean methodologies affects MSMEs and workforce efficiency in the Indian environment. Thus, the goal of this study is to identify areas for further research on lean implementation. The following sections will focus on, first, that more research should be conducted to examine lean implementation in MSMEs using real-time practical database research and combined methods, followed by geographic theory. These approaches provide insight into the complexity of lean implementation in MSMEs. Second, most previous lean studies were in favour of western countries, and they have neglected developing countries like India. A practical execution and a comparative case study of MSMEs employing lean in various industrial sectors across the nation are valuable research areas that provide light on the application of lean technologies in India. Thirdly, although lean has traditionally been studied at the academic level, its growing importance in MSMEs demands further research.

The areas for further research become apparent from the 'categories' literature review. It was obvious that prior studies had mainly concentrated on the theoretical aspect and some methods used to implement Lean in SMEs. Further, focusing on soft issues is needed, for example, those influenced by organisational factors, rather than on technical issues on why selected tools and techniques were chosen. The current research work is focused on fuzzy AHP tools and some cultural change through lean management techniques. The uniqueness of the tools helped to explore MSMEs' issues concerned with practical execution on the ground to strengthen their strategies for operational transformations. Additionally, the research work has also focused on areas such as why lean is adopted by MSMEs, how it is assimilated into their existing strategies, and how lean influences business growth. The research work has also been carried out on the operational benefits that go beyond developments and improvements, making SMEs operationally capable of producing more to contribute more to India's GDP.

1.6.3. Identification of Lean Tools and Practices

Commonly, the effects of the five most vital lean practices were analysed in the literature: Continuous Improvement (CI), Pull Production System (PPS), Heijunka, Value Stream Mapping (VSM), and Total Productive Maintenance (TPM), on contemporary measures of lean performance. Findings indicated that Heijunka had the most substantial impact on operational performance, CI, TPM, and VSM. According to research, the correlation between lean principles and operational performance has been quantitatively proven. Better lean planning and tool selection would benefit from research. Yadav and associates defined lean practices as the total elimination of waste from the system, wherever it exists. The streamlined flow of information, material, and continuous improvement in all system parts were cited as critical lean practices to achieve perfection. Kaizen (a Japanese philosophy of continuous improvement), Poka-Yoke, and Cellular Manufacturing (CM) were cited as critical lean practices towards attaining the targeted level of leanness.

According to a recent study, a lean root map was developed in 2014 to describe the fundamentals of the lean implementation methodology. One of the essential lean principles recommended was continuous improvement. Practical training, early detection of process problems, proper development of idea management, and an adequate reward and recognition system can all help ensure continuous improvement. Various practices of lean implementation, such as 5S, VSM, Poka-Yoke (mistake proofing), Kanban, JIT (Just in Time), etc., were analysed for gear shaft manufacturing companies. VSM was identified as a critical lean practice in various industrial environments. The value of takt time was stressed during the value stream mapping process to align production with demand, leading to manufacturing excellence and significant enhancements in the productivity of SMEs in the machine tool sector. 5S, VSM, and Kanban have been successfully applied to reduce lead time and in-process inventory in the Indian bearing industry, significantly enhancing productivity. VSM, combined with other lean tools such as Five Why and Ishikawa or fishbone diagrams, was successfully applied in various manufacturing and services industries to reduce lead time and in-process inventory. Method time measurement and line balancing were successfully used in the truck body assembly line to reduce bottlenecks and cycle time in the system.

Lean practices such as waste elimination, Kaizen, VSM, JIT, Pull, Cross-Functional Team (CFT), decentralised responsibilities, integrated functions, and vertical information systems were implemented in the kitchenware industry to achieve considerable improvement in all contemporary performance parameters. Kaizen and single-piece flow were applied to reduce cycle time and inventory and increase visibility in the crankshaft assembly line system. Total Productive Maintenance was implemented in the machine shop to enhance machine availability performance and improve the quality yield. A combination of lean practices and tools such as Total Productive Maintenance, Total Quality Management, Failure Mode and Effect Analysis, 5S, Quality Function Deployment, Kaizen, Kanban, and Value Stream Mapping was used as inputs to structural equation modelling to determine the various dimensions of lean manufacturing. Simulation and value stream mapping were used to design a lean production system for doors and windows manufacturers following the job shop production system. The seventeen lean practices and lean tools, namely CFT, QC, set-up time reduction, 5S, Kanban, Continuous Flow, PM (Preventive Maintenance), Small Lot Size, Total Quality Control (TQC), Standard Operational Training, Kaizen, Cellular Layout, Focused Factory, Visual Management and Control, Supplier Management, and Teamwork, were emphasised as crucial elements for effectively implementing lean practices in small and medium-sized enterprises (SMEs). According to a Malaysian study, the Kanban system was the most critical lean methodology for successful lean implementation in Malaysian SMEs. In Indian SMEs, Value Stream Mapping, Total Productive Maintenance (TPM), Kanban, 5S, Single-Minute Exchange of Die (SMED), and Poka-Yoke can eliminate waste and increase production. According to a research study and subsequent statistical analysis, continuous improvement, workplace organisation, and standardisation were the most essential and widely adopted lean techniques in Malaysian automotive SMEs. Malaysian manufacturers also conducted an exploratory factor analysis to find the most critical lean factors. Process optimisation, layout, and working practices were determined as lean factors. A collection of nine fundamental lean practices was suggested as a starting point for lean implementation to improve the firm's overall performance, regardless of size. These practices were focused on identifying and eliminating waste. The aims of various essential lean tools are described in Table 1.

Improper lean tool selection and a lack of lean implementation methodology have been identified as significant challenges to SMEs implementing lean philosophy. Different lean techniques were suggested and found feasible in various manufacturing environments, as expressed by the review of literature, although many of the lean practices cited were overlapping and confusing in nature. A comprehensive study was recently conducted in India to identify various lean elements and associated lean variables that are possible in the Indian SMEs automotive sector. The table below (Table 2) lists several lean factors and associated lean variables for Indian automotive SMEs, which served as the foundation for a thorough evaluation of the leanness of Indian automotive SMEs.

1.6.4. Lean Measurement System

Several systems are developed to check the degree of leanness; some of them are Factory Fundamental Activities (FFA), an assessment technique to determine the level of Lean Practices in any manufacturing and non-manufacturing unit. It also reflects the degree of manufacturing/services excellence in an organization. Before we take measures to implement Manufacturing Excellence in an organization, we must conduct an assessment first. FFA Assessment thus is an initial phase of Manufacturing/Operations Excellence activities. This assessment is carried out through a well-researched HFA software, which focuses on six parameters. Many questions, which cover all aspects of an organization's current fundamental-level operations, are to be answered by the zone/sub-zone leaders. It has been found that if 60 percent to 65 percent of these questionnaires are answered affirmatively – "Yes," the units are on their way to a significant fundamental transformation. In simple words, it means there is good involvement of employees, and they are engaged in micro-level activities related to their operations. The FFA's six key elements are – 5S, Visual Management and Visual Control, Resource Maintainability, Kaizen Improvement, Standardization, and Process Focus.

A slack-based lean measurement system based on linear programming was developed with benchmarking to quantify the degree of leanness, commonly known as the lean score. The lean score measures how much value is added and how waste is reduced through different lean practices. The model for assessing lean practices was created using fuzzy set theory, focusing on five critical parameters for the Indian auto component industry. A fuzzy logic-based theoretical lean measurement system comprising three levels – lean enabler, lean criteria, and lean attribute – was suggested, followed by gap analysis. To enhance the efficiency of our manufacturing organization, we have developed a mathematical lean measurement model. This model allows us to identify weak lean criteria and implement corrective measures to reduce waste. By assessing the effectiveness of different lean strategies, we aim to improve the overall leanness of our organization. This model helped identify a suitable lean strategy for manufacturing organizations (Soriano & Forrester, 2002). A survey-based method was used to evaluate the operational performance of various manufacturing firms that have implemented lean philosophy in all four geographic regions in India. About 80% of the firms implemented lean practices such as customer focus, JIT, SMED, statistical process control, TPM, and cross-functional problem-solving. Implementing these lean practices improved productivity and reduced lead time, inventory, and space requirements (Ghosh, 2012). The fuzzy logic-based advisory system was formulated to help SMEs avoid poor implementation decisions. The system is intended to measure the lean readiness of the organization. The degree of lean readiness determines the various resources needed and has a vital bearing on the success or failure of a lean implementation program (Achanga et al., 2012). The lean model that considers the various lean principles was developed. A framework for evaluating the cost-effectiveness of various lean tools was developed, applying multi-criteria decision-making. The model was developed with a deep knowledge of the change process in lean implementation, aiming to reduce uncertainty and vagueness. It also offered essential insights into how adding or removing a specific lean tool impacts leanness and, consequently, the company's operational performance. The lean framework was developed with the help of the Deming and Kaizen cycle. Quality function deployment, value stream mapping, and balanced scorecard were applied to measure the cost-effectiveness of lean tools concerning customer requirements and the issues related to implementation (Alsyouf et al., 2011).

1.7. Hypothesis

Given the above objectives, the following hypotheses are framed:

- The MSME sector exports outperformed the total exports from India in the post-liberalization period (2005–20).
- The share of MSME exports has increased after the economic reforms of the Indian economy.

1.8. Chapter Scheme

The study has been split into seven chapters, including the current one. The second chapter looks into the concept of Lean and Micro, Small, and Medium Enterprises in the Indian context. The same chapter concentrates on the approach and performance of the Lean management system in industries. It also makes a comparative analysis of small- and large-scale industry sectors.

The third chapter focuses on the growth and performance evaluation of India's MSMEs, utilizing lean tools and practices, and lean measurement systems and models. The fourth chapter, the core chapter of our study, concentrates on developing an integrated lean model and its practices in various MSMEs in India. The fifth chapter analyses the export performance of the small and medium industries sector vis-à-vis the total exports from India. It also deals with the export trend of principal commodities from the small-scale industry sector and the total exports of these commodities from India. The second-last chapter tries to identify the problems and prospects of MSME exports from India and gives measures to promote exports from this sector. The final chapter summarizes the study, includes a SWOT analysis, and concludes.

Chapter 2 | Lean in MSME: An Indian Experience

2.1. Introduction

Since the post-economic reform, India has grown and developed economically, but still, we appear to lag behind many developed and developing nations. From the export perspective, China has surprised us all and has emerged as the world leader in practically all sectors. China alone has been enough to threaten larger export units in the USA and Europe, particularly in the auto, electronics, telecom, steel, and engineering sectors.

India has also grown relatively, but differently from expectations. Our mixed economy model encouraged public sector investments, provided significant-scale employment, and helped develop backward areas. However, it could not tap into India's abundant potential in terms of available human resources, natural resources, and vast coastline. Thus, our MSMEs' export contribution to the GDP could not rise to the expected level. Their contribution to global markets has also been relatively marginal, except in the IT industry. There are many political, social, and economic reasons behind this. It will be beyond our scope to elaborate on them. A lot has been done since the post-economic reform and still, much remains to be done.

India's situation, perhaps, is quite different and unique. Here are some facts about India:

- A large presence of 64 million SMEs (accounting for 17.4% of India's GDP), employing 60 million people (40% of the total workforce).
- These SMEs are responsible for 45% of our country's manufacturing output and 40% of our total exports.
- 17% of SMEs are classified as part of the services sector, which accounts for 56.5% of GDP.
- 95% of SMEs are proprietorships/partnerships.
- Around 72% of the units employ under 50 people.
- Less than 350 factories employ more than 5,000 people.

- A large presence of an unorganised manufacturing sector, as over 90% of SMEs belong to unorganised and unregistered segments.
- 50% of the SMEs are run by disadvantaged groups in our society and hence play a vital role in inclusive growth.
- Poor infrastructural support from the government, like roads, transportation, power, and water, despite some serious recent efforts by the government.
- Too many old laws for control, too many inspectors, and too many checks and balances. The ease of doing business is difficult, though the government, through various programs, is trying to ease these problems.
- Low productivity, unskilled manpower, and not as disciplined as one sees in Japan, the USA, China, etc.
- High cost of investment and working capital. Interest rates are high.
- Inadequate support from the government on R&D, technology upgradation, skill development, training, marketing, and procurement.
- Too much tax burden due to multiple tax slabs.
- Corruption at various levels, now particularly at the lower levels.

Even a large sector has its share of problems. Managerial talent is highly mobile and unstable. About 80% of the workforce is contractual and temporary, thus creating typical problems at the bottom due to a lack of commitment. The quality of the work environment, which ensures productive output, has gone missing. Realising the situation we are in, our government, under the leadership of our dynamic Prime Minister, Mr. Narendra Modi, has announced several new initiatives like Swachh Bharat, Digital India (DI), Make in India (MI), Skill India (SI), Startup India, Housing for All by 2022, and the Pradhan Mantri Dhan Yojana. Initiatives have been taken on lean manufacturing for global competitiveness for the MSMEs through a cluster approach. And now, ZED – Zero Defect - Zero Effect campaign – is also being launched.

2.2. Make in India Campaign

The Government's *Make in India* programme has set its sights on turning the country into a prominent manufacturing powerhouse on the global stage by focusing on enhancing infrastructure and simplifying the business landscape. The objective is to increase manufacturing's contribution to the GDP from 15% to 25%. This national programme encourages investment, protects intellectual property, and establishes state-of-the-art manufacturing facilities.

2.3. Objectives of the Make in India Programme

The primary objective behind the 'Make in India' plan is to make jobs available in India by focusing on public enterprise and heavy industries.

The government has placed a strong emphasis on the framework, highlighting its time-bound project clearances through a single online portal. Moreover, they have assigned an eight-member team to cater to investor queries within 72 hours while also addressing critical issues such as labour laws, skill development, and infrastructure.

India's high-value manufacturing sectors will benefit from the easing of investment ceilings and limitations – defence, construction, and railways will be open to international participation.

The industrial sectors that will benefit from this campaign are: automobiles, automobile components, aviation, biotechnology, defence manufacturing, electrical equipment and machinery, electronics, chemicals, construction, food processing, IT and BPM, leather, media, mining, oil and gas, pharmaceuticals, ports, and many more.

With fresh investments in the larger sector, MSMEs, as support, will get a definite boost and play a significant role in India's economy.

2.4. Some Benefits Announced for Msmes Are As Under

2.4.1. Technology Development

- Incentives to produce equipment/technical devices/machineries for mitigating pollution, minimising energy consumption, and conserving water.

- MSMEs will be granted access to the patent pool, and part of the compensation for technology procurement costs will be provided, up to a ceiling of INR 20 lakhs for acquiring suitable technologies over a maximum time frame of 5 years.

2.4.2. Special Advantages to MSMEs

- Individuals who reinvest the earnings from the sale of residential property are eligible for relief on long-term capital gains tax.
- Taxation that allows pass-through tax status for venture capital funds focused on Small and Medium Enterprises (SMEs) in the manufacturing sector.
- The Reserve Bank of India guidelines for banks investing in venture capital funds centred on small and medium-sized industries have been relaxed, in consultation with the RBI.
- The relaxation of IRDA regulations to allow investments by insurance firms.
- The provision of loans to MSMEs, especially in the manufacturing sector, falls under priority lending.
- Easier access to bank funding through appropriate lending standards.
- Establishing a stock exchange for MSMEs.
- Service industries dedicated to the management and payment of legal dues of MSMEs.

Thus, it is evident that MSME is a priority sector now. To make this sector globally competitive, a highly subsidised Lean Cluster Scheme, conceived by the National Manufacturing Competitive Council, was initiated by the Ministry of MSME with implementation support from the National Productivity Council (NPC) and the Quality Council of India (QCI). The prime objective of this scheme and initiatives is to make MSME sector manufacturing companies globally competitive through the execution of Lean Manufacturing concepts, which have majorly been derived from the highly successful and famous Toyota Production System of Toyota Motor Corporation, Japan. As the target companies are small, the cluster approach was conceived as the best suitable model for Lean Implementation for small companies.

2.5. Lean Manufacturing Competitiveness for MSMEs

The "Lean Manufacturing Competitiveness Scheme" was launched by the Development Commissioner, Ministry of MSMEs, to enhance the competitiveness of Micro, Small and Medium-sized enterprises. At the beginning, it was started as a pilot scheme for 100 mini-clusters in 2009, and the upscaled scheme received approval for 500 mini-clusters in the year 2013.

The scheme is initiated through mini-clusters as Special Purpose Vehicles (SPVs) comprising 8–12 units per cluster. Each mini-cluster is supported by an empanelled Lean Manufacturing Consultant (LMC), who plays a crucial role in implementing lean tools and techniques. The government grant covers up to 80 percent of the LMC consultancy fees, with the remaining 20 percent of the cost being covered by the SPVs/units. The implementation period spans 18 months, divided into five incremental stages.

The primary rationale of the Indian Government to help MSMEs adopt the Lean Manufacturing System (LMS) is to enhance their productivity and competitiveness by minimising process wastes in areas such as quality improvement, inventory management, space optimisation, energy consumption, etc. The application of LMS techniques also reduces manufacturing parts rejection, process set-up time and standardisation, and creates a better machine layout, which helps reduce excess transportation and motion during the manufacturing processes. The proper implementation of LMS techniques facilitates cost savings for MSMEs. Additionally, there are a number of social benefits including manpower training, knowledge bank creation, increased labour productivity, reduced input costs for other industries, the introduction of innovative production tools and methods in manufacturing, and the fostering of a rich work culture in society.

The implementation of LMS techniques in the organisation will result in increased return to scale, which includes (i) economy of scale that lowers the per unit production cost, (ii) heightened productivity inside the organisation, and (iii) improved competitiveness in both the domestic and global markets. At the same time, this leads to enhanced expertise in the company in respect of improved workplace culture, managerial skills, and so on. The initiatives also lead to the "demonstration effect." Some enterprises have already initiated LMS practices and have started to enjoy the associated advantages, but these practices have not yet reached many MSMEs in the country. The principles and methods of lean manufacturing are still unfamiliar to most of the MSMEs in the country.

Manufacturing has been identified as the primary driver of economic growth. The contribution of the Indian manufacturing sector to its GDP has plateaued at 14–15% only. The National Manufacturing Policy of the Government of India envisages a contribution of manufacturing to reach 25 percent of the country's GDP by the end of 2022. To achieve sustainable growth, the manufacturing segment needs to build and maintain the competitiveness required to face the challenges posed by globalisation. The LMS scheme will help MSMEs lower their units' making costs through better workload balancing, optimum space utilisation, better inventory management, optimised process flow, reduced process lead times, etc. To support the initiatives, the Indian government established the Excellence Awards in Lean Implementation in 2013. The SMEs will be urged to enter the competition and compete for the national award.

2.6. Need for Lean Manufacturing

The dynamic global environment has made it difficult for all the components in the economy to remain competitive and survive. The manufacturing industries, especially MSMEs, have felt the impact more significantly. It has been observed that units are so preoccupied with day-to-day management concerns that they don't have sufficient time and resources to focus on developing a strategic insight into the need for and acquisition of different methods that would help them increase their productivity and, as a result, be competitive in global markets. The Lean Manufacturing System is a set of methods that has developed over time and considers several minor breakthroughs that aid in cost reduction and, as a result, boost efficiency and competitive edge. Below is a list of the key LM techniques, along with a brief overview of each:

- **5S System:** The 5S system is workplace management, which helps eliminate "wastes" from the workplace and sets standard operating procedures (SOPs) to maintain it. 5S is an acronym for Sort, Set-in-order, Shine, Standardise and Sustain.

- **Visual Control (VC):** Visual management and controls such as charts, cartoons, light signals, walkway markings on the floor, warning signs, demarcation of zones, safety instructions, Poka-Yoke instructions, etc., can be placed across the workplace.
- **Standard Operating Procedures (SOPs):** Each verbal directive must be transformed into an SOP to minimise dependency on skilled personnel and achieve the desired product quality, consistency, effectiveness, and efficiency.
- **Just in Time (JIT):** JIT is a Japanese philosophy focused on making the required product in the desired amount at the right time. This approach almost eliminates inventory and achieves the shortest possible cycle time.
- **KANBAN System:** Under this system, parts are drawn from the assembly or the next workstation, and the bin with the correct quantities is replenished by the previous work centre. This helps to minimise excess inventory of components.
- **Cellular Layout:** In modern manufacturing circumstances, we focus on completing components within smaller self-contained cells, which are part of a larger factory. This approach contrasts with the traditional functional layout, where completion is based on specific operations.
- **Value Stream Mapping (VSM):** It encompasses all activities—value added (VA), non-value added (NVA), and essential non-value added (ENVA)—and assists in arriving at the optimal layout of all resources needed for making the product.
- **Poka-Yoke:** This Japanese method results in a "Zero Defect" state by preventing defects from occurring at their point of origin.
- **Quick Changeover:** Using innovative techniques, setup time is reduced to under ten minutes, facilitating the manufacturing of smaller quantities as demanded by the customer.
- **Total Productive Maintenance (TPM):** It started as a method of physical asset management focused on maintaining and

improving manufacturing equipment to reduce the operating cost of an organisation.

- **Kaizen Blitz:** The goal of a kaizen blitz, often referred to as a kaizen event, is to find opportunities for improvement in a business process and quickly apply proven solutions that are successful.

The program is an initiative to enhance the manufacturing sector's competitiveness. This program offers the optimal setting for conducting and collecting various case studies to analyze lean execution in MSMEs.

Lean offers a way to do more with fewer of everything – less human effort, less equipment required, fewer expenses for operations, less time, and less operational space – while aiming at continuous improvement (CI) and customer satisfaction. Considering the volatile business environment and hyper-competition, adopting and practicing lean helps improve production systems and move up the value delivery chain. Indian MSMEs often operate in reactive mode, lacking a proactive approach towards productivity and growth. Lean provides a solution for crisis management and supports the adoption of a culture of continuous improvement across operational practices.

To gain insight into the lean experience in India, various studies from primary literature sources such as Emerald Insight, Science Direct, Taylor and Francis, KPMG, Deloitte, Report on MSMEs Govt. of India, etc., were examined. Many of these studies were conducted within the last five years (excluding COVID time), which could possibly be conceived as a result of lean management's popularity in response to competition and the growing focus on emerging economies. Most of the research has been conducted in the manufacturing sector; hence, lean penetration is mainly limited to traditional industries.

The study indicates that lean has emerged as an optional model for MSMEs in developing countries over the past decade. The recent literature reflects a comparable moment with the expansion of lean manufacturing practices to MSMEs in India. This can be attributed to the need for adopting operational strategies that cater to big organizations and address competitive pressures. However, the acceptance of executing lean methodologies by Indian MSMEs is a little complicated but essential due to their distinct operational and managerial characteristics.

2.7. Lean Implementation Methodology

A pilot study is a systematic investigation of an event or set of connected events aimed at describing the phenomenon being examined. Research through pilot studies in operations management has contributed significantly to the development of breakthrough concepts. It facilitates the development of new principles and theories, the testing and refinement of existing approaches, and provides new insights and perspectives. One significant advantage of conducting research in the field is its ability to enhance validity with practitioners and consultants by addressing real issues and considering the attitudes of individuals at all levels of the organization.

Additionally, case studies are increasingly prevalent in operations management systems since they make it easier to comprehend the linkages between tangible and intangible issues within the organization. Given the circumstances, the pilot study approach was deemed the most appropriate for this research.

Various methodologies have been adopted earlier; among them, the SAP-LAP framework has been utilized in the present study due to its flexible application. Traditional frameworks like SWOT and PEST analysis are generally more static than the SAP-LAP model, which goes beyond merely identifying the issue to also include discussion on how to effect change to bridge the gap between expectations and outcomes.

The SAP-LAP analysis serves as a framework for learning and interpretation. It has gained popularity as a very useful model of investigation in operations management.

The Situation, Actor, and Process are fundamental elements of any organizational framework. Through the process, the actor navigates the situation. This interaction between the members leads to insights or the acquisition of new knowledge. The wide learning and deep understanding thus developed would lead to appropriate actions, resulting in adequate outcomes for the system. Feedback regarding performance gaps would provide further learning and control measures.

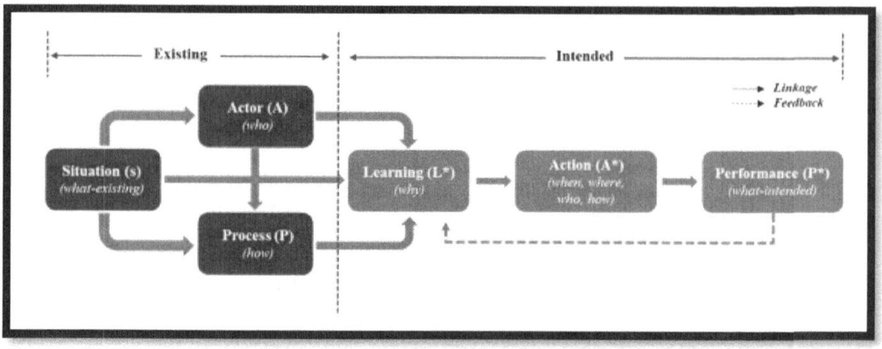

Figure 2.1: SAP-LAP Foundation

SAP-LAP Foundation	
Level	**Query**
Situation	What is going on at the moment? What is anticipated to occur? What are the major opportunities and challenges?
Actor	What roles and capabilities do the actor demonstrate? In which area can once exercise their freedom of choice?
Process	What actions currently being taken? What method being used? What is the reason to carried out? What all factors involved?
Learning	What are the key issues associated with the situation? What are the key issues related to the participants? What are the key issues associated with the process?
Action	What action can be taken to improve the situation? What action can be taken to improve the actors? What steps can be taken to improve the process?
Performance	What effect will the situation have? What impact will the actors experienced? In what forms the performance of the process be enhanced?

Table 2.1: SAP-LAP Foundation

SAP-LAP's holistic approach and adaptability to any organizational context are advantages. They allow for innovative thinking and in-depth analysis.

The present study offered insight into lean adoption by organizations that participated in the 'Lean Competitiveness Scheme' using the SAP-LAP structure.

The research questions that will be explored in the pilot study are:

- How has the proper implementation of lean practices in Indian MSMEs contributed to mitigating environmental challenges, threats, and overcoming existing organizational weaknesses?
- Who all are the significant players in lean implementation in Indian MSMEs?
- What steps are involved in implementing lean in MSMEs?
- What learnings can be gained from applying lean principles among Indian MSMEs?
- Has the Indian government program achieved the expected outcomes? Is there further potential for enhancing the model?
- Is it possible to apply the lean implementation process outside the scheme?

The strategy for the current research work has been sourced from various reports, research articles, and semi-structured interactions with several empaneled consultants who participated in the LMC scheme. The insights have been enhanced through visits to the various participating organizations across Indian states and workshops organized by the government as well as the Lean Consulting companies. Information regarding the participating companies was obtained from the Quality Council of India (QCI) and the National Productivity Council (NPC), the entities responsible for executing and overseeing the initiatives. The Lean Consultants involved in the various lean projects evaluate the current manufacturing processes of the cluster members and advise them on the adoption of lean techniques. They have dedicated 18 months to collaboration with the organizations through 5 phases. As a result, they possess a unique position of having unrestrained access to the intricate details of the organizational operations.

The SAP-LAP structure has been developed based on information taken from various linkages and the collective exposures of various lean manufacturing consultants who have completed cluster projects.

2.8. SAP-LAP Framework

2.8.1. Situation

MSMEs in India hold significant potential to form the backbone of the economy. Their inputs to GDP, exports, and employment make them a focus area for the growth and development of India. Given the importance of small and medium-sized industries, the government has introduced many schemes to encourage inclusive growth, focusing on credit availability, technology upgrades, marketing support, and quality improvement. The 'Make in India' initiative is another massive step toward promoting and fostering confidence in the Indian manufacturing sector. Despite such measures, a turbulent commercial environment threatens the small and micro sectors. India encounters strong competition from China, Taiwan, and Bangladesh. The implementation of demonetization in 2016 and the GST rollout in 2017 significantly affected manufacturing MSMEs, which have faced challenges in adapting to these changes. It is essential to adopt good practices and focus on waste reduction. This situation has made the adoption of lean manufacturing practices even more imminent.

In addition to the external factors, Indian MSMEs face various obstacles. The organizations are reluctant to share information due to concerns about safeguarding their valuable knowledge and constant pressure from customers to reduce prices and improve quality. There is also a lack of trust between labour and management, causing organizational inefficiency and inhibiting the implementation of improvement programs. Organizational resistance to technological upgradation and improving process methodologies is a significant challenge. The present scenario demands awareness and training on various lean tools and techniques.

2.8.2. Actors

Usually, the motivation for lean adoption in India comes from external sources, i.e., the government or the customer. However, top management is the catalyst for lean transformation in any organization. The process involves employing various consultants to help in implementing lean techniques alongside the management team. The lean consultants aim to address the various challenges emerging from the process area and support the organization in achieving lean status. Building trust with the top management team is essential to facilitate change in their operational processes.

The successful transformation happens when management collaborates closely with the lean consultants. While top management holds the authority and is a key player, along with the lean consultants providing guidance, lean practices succeed only when they are executed at the shop floor level. Thus, gaining floor-level employee support is crucial, although this remains a decision for the management authority, which maintains freedom of choice.

2.8.3. Process

The LMCS program requires establishing targets in advance with the approval of the top management and the regulatory bodies (NPC and QCI), which the consultants must achieve.

The entire project is divided into five incremental phases, with an audit conducted after each phase. At the end of the project, the sustenance plan for the next year is decided, which the organizations must adhere to.

Phases of Lean Projects

Phase	Steps
Phase - I	In this phase, projects to be undertaken and KPIs are decided. The diagnostic study, along with the action plan, is done to map the value stream.
Phase - II	The initiation of lean implementation starts with a 5S system, visual management and control, Kaizen (for achieve total employee engagement), and safety tools, which are standard for all cluster members and do not demand a huge investment.
Phase - III & IV	Organization, along with the process-specific projects are undertaken in this phase.
Phase - V	Project completion reports and the deadline and the target. It is expected to be completed by phase V, and the financial savings will be realized by then.

Table 2.2: Phases of Lean Projects

Based on the diagnostic study carried out in phase 1, the problematic area of the factory is identified and addressed first, followed by the entire factory. The improvement and upgradation in the highly impacted areas serve as a catalyst for a more seamless implementation across the factory. This approach also boosts confidence in the initiatives.

In an ideal scenario, Lean management and execution teams should consist of a minimum of 30 percent representation from each department. Additionally, a Lean coordinator is designated to coordinate and manage the task with the Lean consultants. The as-is condition photography at the time of the diagnostic study helps in monitoring improvement.

The first impact of a streamlined process in the factory is that it becomes more 'Visual,' meaning the visual improvement through 5S, visual management and control, and raising employee awareness regarding the NVA or the waste.

During the on-ground Lean project, more emphasis is placed on complete employee engagement. Initiatives such as suggestion programs, Quality Circles, and continual improvement and Kaizen reward schemes are implemented to guarantee the highest level of participation. The Lean project cannot be executed independently; it must be integrated into the operational process with the support of all the stakeholders at every level. Hence, Lean implementation practices encompass not just the Lean project team but also include all employees across the organization.

The procedures serve as a broad representation of the process followed by the consultants as part of the Lean Manufacturing Competitiveness Scheme.

2.8.4. Learning

Lean should be understood as "Least Efforts Are Needed" across the entire value chain. It offers solutions to most of the MSMEs' perennial problems, like scarce resources and customer pressures to enhance quality while bringing down operational costs.

The adoption of Lean diffusion in India's auto component sector is remarkably higher than in non-auto component manufacturing sectors, as it has been primarily customer-driven. Automotive OEMs (Original

Equipment Manufacturers) have stressed the importance of Lean manufacturing practices and encouraged their suppliers to execute Lean methodology. This has resulted in greater acceptance of Lean principles and practices among auto-manufacturing sectors within Indian MSMEs that serve as tier-1, tier-2, and tier-3 suppliers.

The success stories from indigenous communities are very important to encourage industries to embrace Lean methodologies, as most organizations feel that Lean methodology does not apply to them because of its Japanese origin. Also, management often misinterprets Lean techniques as solely an on-floor initiative, thus resulting in the shortcoming of comprehensive adoption across the organization and finally leading to its failure. Consequently, they assign accountability for it to lower-tier management.

There are a few mini clusters started under the scheme that are only sometimes 'business clusters,' which leads to challenges in execution and creates barriers to knowledge sharing among the cluster members.

The significant presence of contractual workers hinders the imbibing of an organization's Lean culture.

Human resources are an organization's most significant asset and change agent. The success factors and sustainability of existing tools and techniques solely depend on skilled human resources. Emphasis should be placed on SoL Lean, which involves techniques and analytical tools. This segment represents a crucial opportunity for enhancement for small and medium-sized enterprises.

2.8.5. Actions

Micro, Small, and Medium Enterprises (MSMEs) suffer from time and resource limitations. For an operational management approach such as Lean to be successfully implemented on the ground, continual training and handholding are dearly required. Below are some recommended steps including:

- The decision-making authority must allot time for the employee to "Think." Regarding the relevance of teamwork activities, Kaizen activities cannot be over-emphasised.
- Sometimes, improvement needs some investment, which later creates an issue—the Lean management consultant faces

difficulty convincing the top management. Keeping focus on quality adds to the direct costs, whereas most of its advantages are implicit, such as customer satisfaction, operational productivity improvement, etc. Facilitating the advantages of quality prioritisation indicates that quality is essential to surpass the competition. Proper time allocation and management for Lean training and education would aid in persuading management and in more straightforward implementation in subsequent phases.

- Indian MSMEs have developed a tendency to reach a crisis as, in most cases, there is a lack of PPC (Production Planning and Control).
- Preliminary audits should be conducted to grasp the actual factory fundamentals. Executing Lean practices on the ground can only succeed if there are changes in culture and overall employee engagement within the organization.
- For the organization to motivate consultants to participate actively in Lean projects, they should adopt the WIIFM "What Is In It For Me" approach.

The sustenance phase needs to be incorporated into the Lean project to ensure that Lean efforts continue beyond the conclusion of the project.

Material Management (MM) and Inventory Control (IC) are highly sensitive areas in Indian MSMEs. Just-in-Time (JIT) and Kanban (the ticketing system) are not properly implemented, as suppliers and customer relations are also not developed enough to support the implementation of these tools. The initiative can significantly improve operational efficiency and free up funds for inventory investment.

"Train the trainer" – there is a shortage of Lean experts who can offer significant importance and support to Indian MSMEs.

2.8.6. Performance

LMCS represents a significant advancement toward assisting MSMEs in gaining a competitive advantage and imbibing a culture of continuous improvement. MSMEs with limited financial resources can begin their lean journey with the government's aid and the consultants' expertise.

Being a part of the program should be seen as a significant movement forward in a lean management journey.

During 2014–2018, around 658 awareness programs were conducted, and more than 456 SPVs were formed. There has been continuous dialogue regarding the potential improvement in the program, given the benefits it offers. A total of 15 KPIs, recognized during the pre-diagnostic and the diagnostic study conducted in the first phase of the lean management project for the participating organizations, provide a clear guideline to the organizations. The initiation of lean projects, accompanied by diagnostic reports, has prompted various industries to diagnose their current situation, showing current situations and areas requiring key focus.

Key Performance Indicators

KPIs enlisted as a part of the Diagnostic Study Report	
KPIs	
Manpower Productivity	Lead Time
Capital Productivity	Value Added Ratio
Annual Savings	On-Time Delivery
Quality Parameters Performance	Throughput Yield
Inventory Turnover	Equipment Availability
Kaizen Implemented	Existing Equipment Efficiency
R&R from Customers	The Floor area optimization
HR Development	

Table 2.3: Key Performance Indicators

The participants' success in the scheme launched can boost MSMEs' morale to adopt a lean philosophy.

It has been observed that the most problematic area in small and medium-sized enterprises is usually managing human resources. The MSMEs hired unskilled, semi-skilled, or freshers at a low cost and have a considerable workload. The employees frequently change organisations for better opportunities; hence, the lean management consultant has to provide hands-on experience again from the basics. The adoption of lean with total engagement at each level would ensure that organisational machinery stays intact despite fluctuations in internal and external environments. The tools and techniques used are only the means and not the ends to achieve the desired outcomes.

The auto manufacturing sector is leading the way in lean manufacturing transformation in India. Focusing on additional sectors, such as apparel, process industries, and electronics, to implement lean practices would enhance the overall performance of the MSME sector.

Better coordination among management, consultants, and the Indian government would help create a positive environment. Organisations should aim to develop a lean mindset rather than merely displaying lean on paper.

2.9. Discussion

SAP-LAP model integrates complex and smooth thinking by working together to blend learning, action, and performance. In the current research work, the model considers the improvement in manufacturing processes in Indian MSMEs by taking advantage of lean management techniques from the perspectives of participating members. The research model helps out in clarifying the various stages involved in executing a lean approach, taking into account both the internal and external circumstances, awarding the various complexities that come up during the implementation process, and aims to provide in-depth and appropriate measures to be implemented.

The Indian manufacturing industries have significant potential because of domestic demand, engineering talent, an increasing youth population, and favourable government schemes. India's MSME segment is one of the prominent and dynamic sectors. It boosts entrepreneurial activities and innovation while serving as an auxiliary to large-scale units. It is essential for MSMEs to adjust themselves in order to align with the demands of customers and implement a new-age operation management system to gain a competitive advantage and survive in today's competitive markets.

Lean management has become one of the most effective operational paradigms of the 21st century. The applicability of lean principles and approaches in Indian MSMEs is even greater as they are moving through a growth phase. Thus, they must streamline their operational processes to better utilise their existing capacity.

The SAP has resulted in various learning challenges regarding the implementation of lean management practices in MSMEs. Some weak areas are human resources management, inventory control, and the requirement for documentation. Based on these critical learning issues, corrective actions can be proposed to address these issues and increase the efficiencies of lean manufacturing practices within the organisation.

Because of their investment in production systems and equipment as well as their limited resources, manufacturing MSMEs experienced on the ground have reduced flexibility. Approaches like lean help them gain adaptability in product volume and varieties. Lean techniques help these micro and small organisations to move out of contradiction mode. A fundamental problem highlighted by the lean consultants was that most industries need to keep inventory on track, manpower productivity, sales trends, etc.; the operations are carried out based on authentic and very precise data. The measurement of all the changes is essential and must continue for more efficient management, and a lean operation model clarifies most issue areas by necessitating baseline data to deliver appropriate solutions. It demands measuring and monitoring of performance. The participant organisations' experiences demonstrate that awareness of the value of inventory in stock helps organisations to eliminate surplus. Similarly, tracking labour productivity and efficiency helps to manage human resources better. The additional benefits were the ergonomic interventions implemented by the lean consultants, significantly improving labour productivity. This aspect had not yet been addressed by the leadership of the organisations. The basic changes in layout have also helped with shorter lead times and better space optimisation.

This scheme allows MSMEs to take advantage by adopting lean as a management system rather than just a project. The hope is that the benefits accrued through lean will propel these organisations toward global competitiveness.

In India, the common types of organisations are one-person and family-operated businesses. In such scenarios, any process improvement initiatives must follow a top-to-bottom approach for making it successful on the ground. It became clear that the effectiveness of lean activity within the mini clusters was possible when management was convinced of its advantages. The primary obstacle is that lean execution requires time and resources, with no immediate results. It becomes crucial for the leaders within the organisation to realise the significance of lean principles and set appropriate expectations.

Lean organisations rely on well-drafted SOPs, reducing dependence on an organisation's single individual. This addresses challenges stemming from labour turnover. It focuses on the importance of 'respect for people,' which results in a better workplace culture. It ensures operational stability through tools like TPM and mistake-proofing. Thus, it has demonstrated itself to be a healthy management system, especially in the uncertain external environment.

Focusing on skill enhancement and soft skills such as employee engagement, problem solving, and a healthy relationship with the supplier and customer are essential considerations. The reference further emphasised the need for management involvement, employee engagement, collaborative problem solving, and continuous improvement for successful lean implementation on the ground.

A culture within the organisation that supports lean initiatives would guarantee their continued success beyond the scheme. Alignment between organisational culture and lean management is essential for efficiency improvement.

Another suggestion was to partner with universities to start relevant courses in operations management to meet the demand for specialists in the field. The integrated skill development centres and vocational training programmes in the operations field would generate a skilled workforce that can be employed directly in these organisations.

Therefore, the spread of lean management practices in India is necessary to enhance its operational efficiency and move towards becoming a global manufacturing hub. The MSME initiatives offer micro and small enterprises an at-par opportunity to maximise their contributions to India's GDP.

The lean management system is a robust operational improvement methodology, but to realise and sustain its advantage, manufacturing MSMEs must overcome challenges such as:

- Leadership challenges such as lack of support, lack of long-term mission and vision, and lack of technical expertise to know how.
- Various challenges inside the organisation, like the lack of employee engagement, an organisational culture to support the same, and human resources concerns such as a high turnover rate and employee well-being.
- Other issues include inventory mismanagement and control, lack of proper documentation, and maintaining a healthy relationship with the supplier and the customer.

2.10. Conclusion and Implications

The SAP-LAP model allows for a concise presentation of the current state of the manufacturing MSMEs, the gap identification in lean implementation, and recommendations for improving operational performance. This study would be beneficial for the stakeholders involved, i.e., including management, lean consultants, and government, by proposing an appropriate measure to improve the operational efficiency of the MSMEs. Operations managers are concerned with achieving an improved state with minimal resources.

The study in the chapter emphasizes that weakness persists despite lean actions taken and advancements made so far. Understanding the advantage of lean principles and practices on the ground would encourage organizations to adopt lean as a way of life. A better understanding of a situational element would help operations managers effectively apply operational improvement methodology successfully. In India, the Government initiative has provided an opportunity for the MSMEs to execute lean, which is a significant step toward enhancing their operational efficiency; it would be wise to analyze and evaluate the success of the scheme to make certain that the available resources can be allocated to the most critical areas that require focus, such as the development of soft skills, ergonomic interventions, integration of the value chain, technological advancement, etc.

The SAP-LAP model allows the integration of both hard as well as soft issues during the execution of lean practices in MSMEs. The pilot study contributes to the existing knowledge base by emphasizing the importance of highlighting the easiest dimensions during the utilization of process improvement initiatives. The research study also reveals the process of executing lean in MSMEs. The lean methodology followed by the consultants across the five different phases provides a complete outline of the lean implementation methodology in Indian MSMEs. It indicates the tools that require the least investment and are very handy to execute on the ground, such as 5S, Visual Management (VM) and Visual Control (VC), Kaizens, etc., followed by process-oriented projects. It also emphasises the existing barriers in the process so that research can be directed toward overcoming them.

The present pilot study restricts itself exclusively to the perspective of lean consultants and observations by the researcher. The current study only includes organizations that are part of the lean scheme which have been considered for the study. An empirical analysis would assist in validating the outcomes and the challenges associated with generalizing based on the case study. Future research work can include the viewpoint of other stakeholders, i.e., management and government. An empirical analysis of the effects of both hard and soft lean implementation practices on operational efficiencies would be beneficial.

Chapter 3| Lean: Performance Evaluation of India's MSME

3.1. Introduction

Under the new "Make in India" policy, India has become a global manufacturing hub. Many Indian companies are eager to adopt the principles of the lean philosophy to achieve long-term strategic benefits over their competitors. Therefore, developing a comprehensive lean evaluation and management system for Indian Micro, Small, and Medium-sized enterprises became necessary to measure their present lean status and potential improvements. This journey towards lean implementation is a necessity and a possible gateway to significant strategic advantages.

Since their introduction in 1990, the principles of lean philosophy have proven effective in various manufacturing settings globally. They have become a panacea for all manufacturing issues and brought about an increase in improvements in achieving lean manufacturing excellence. However, in most cases, the missions ultimately did not live up to the mark because of the non-judgmental use of various lean principles and practices and the lack of an appropriate measurement mechanism.

According to recent research, manufacturing leanness was possible in Finnish small and medium-sized enterprises. Lean approaches, such as continuous system improvement and waste reduction, were used to achieve efficiency in manufacturing. However, due to the insufficient and customized lean deployment approach, various SMEs failed terribly in their lean journey. Findings suggested that a suitable and customized lean deployment approach could make SMEs more rational in their lean journey of execution, and chances of failure can be reduced. Recognizing potential operational opportunities and weaknesses could make an organization more aware of its competencies and weaknesses. A comprehensive six-phased lean implementation methodology was also proposed. According to the model, the lean implementation program should initiate with a strategic market analysis, which is driven by the customer based on their requirements, followed by forming a cross-functional team, judicial selection of lean tools and techniques, VSM, and others.

Indian SMEs are the prime drivers of the Indian economy and employ millions and millions of people. An excellent lean performance evaluation technique could provide vital clues about their weaknesses in lean tool and method selection and subsequent execution of the same so that they can take appropriate corrective measures to improve leanness and gain a sustainable strategic advantage over their competitors. The current research work concentrated on evaluating the lean implementation performance of Indian SMEs implementing fuzzy AHP.

The research started by exploring various lean factors and related sub-factors, which explain the leanness of the system that is being associated through a literature review. The literature review resulted in the development of a hierarchical structure for the system. The next phase was selecting a suitable weighing method to determine the weight of those identified factors and sub-factors, thereby establishing their relative importance.

The direct ratio approach and methodology are often used to determine the factors and their related sub-factors. The direct ratio method starts with identifying features and related sub-factors. A pairwise comparison is made to determine their relative significance. Lastly, the defined weight must be checked for inconsistency if there is any. However, in a real-world scenario, it is exceptionally challenging to obtain a consistent preference of decision-makers for their personal assessment and anticipate their behaviour to act 100% rationally at all times. Therefore, the direct ratio method will project a degree of consistency (Rommelfanger & Eickemeier, 2013). Finding other methods that can tolerate a certain level of inconsistency and provide foolproof measures for finding inconsistencies is imperative. The AHP stands out as one of the better choices available. It was first introduced by Thomas L. Saaty. AHP allows the assignment of weight by categorizing and breaking down the issues into various hierarchical levels, known as sub-problems. Though the AHP offers a process to assess inconsistencies and allocate weights in a logical and structured way, it has often been critically faced for failing to take care of inaccuracies and uncertainties in decision-making (Tsvetanov &

Mikhailov, 2004; Yang & Chen, 2004). AHP signifies relative importance with a precise number during the pairwise comparison process. However, it can be quite challenging for the evaluator to measure the significance exactly using exact values in a practical situation. The evaluation should be in a set range with minimum, mean, and maximum values. This arrangement is taken into account by the fuzzy set theory. An advanced and extended version of AHP, that is, a fuzzy set AHP procedure, utilizes a nine-point scale along with a triangular fuzzy number to assess the various lean factors that contribute to sustainable strategic advantages for MSMEs in India within the Indian SME environment (Rommelfanger & Eickemeier, 2013). Post-development of the weight index for the complete measurement system, a fuzzy comprehensive analysis was conducted to assess the level of leanness in Indian SMEs.

3.2. Identification of Lean Tools and Practices

The research work has provided statistically proven evidence of a connection between lean management practices and operational efficiencies. Typically, the effects of the key lean practices examined, such as the pull production system (PPS), heijunka (production leveling), CI, TPM, and VSM, on modern lean performance measurements were studied. The outcomes showed that heijunka had the greatest impact on operational performance, along with CI, TPM, and VSM. Yadav and associates described lean practices as the complete elimination of process and system wastes, no matter where they exist. The information and material flow and CIs in all system parts were identified as the essential lean manufacturing practices for reaching out to perfection (Yadav et al., 2010). Kaizen (the continual improvement), cellular manufacturing (CM), and poka-yoke (the mistake proofing) were recognized as the key lean practices for achieving the desired level of leanness (Womack & Jones, 2010). Based on the research work done between 2014 and 2015, a lean manufacturing road map was framed to describe the framework of lean execution (Sundar et al., 2014-15). CI was also facilitated by effective lean training. CI can be targeted and achieved through proper training on the ground, early identification of process abnormality, proper development of lean thinking and brainstorming within the team, and an adequate R&R system.

Different methods of implementing lean methodologies, such as VSM, visual management and control, 5S system, poka-yoke, Kanban, JIT, etc., were analyzed for the different manufacturing and transactional business processes. VSM was recognized as the key lean practice in various industrial environments. The significance of takt time (TT) was focused on through VSM to align production with demand, targeting lean manufacturing excellence and dramatically increasing both manpower and machine productivity in various small- and medium-sized enterprises (Ricondo et al., 2016). VSM, the 5S system, and Kanban have been successfully implemented and studied to reduce process lead time and in-process inventory stock in the Indian manufacturing industry, significantly enhancing productivity. VSM combined with lean tools such as the five whys and the fishbone diagram was successfully applied and studied in the healthcare industry to reduce lead time and in-process inventory stock in the system (Tomas & Martin, 2015). Method time measurement and flow management were successfully executed in various body shop assembly lines to identify and reduce bottlenecks and cycle time in the system (Kumar & Kumar, 2014).

VSM, Kaizen, and single-piece flow (SPF) were successfully implemented to reduce cycle time (CT) and process inventory and to increase visibility in the crankshaft manufacturing line system (Venkataraman, 2014). TPM was executed in the machine shop to increase machine availability and performance and to achieve a better-quality yield. Lean management practices such as waste, Kaizen, JIT, pull, cross-functional teams, decentralized responsibilities, vertical information systems, and integrated functions were executed in the kitchenware industry to achieve a better and remarkable improvement in all contemporary performance parameters. A combination of lean practices and tools such as TPM, Quality Function Deployment (QFD), Total Quality Management (TQM), FMEA, the 5S system, Kaizen, Kanban, and VSM was used as inputs to the structural equation modeling to determine various parameters of lean manufacturing (Vinodh & Joy, 2012). Simulation and VSM were used to make a structure of the lean production system (LPS) for door and window manufacturers following the shop floor production system (Gurumurthy & Kodali, 2011). Seventeen lean practices and lean tools, namely: cross-functional team, quality circle (QC), reduction of setup time, 5S system, Kanban, continuous improvement flow, preventive maintenance (PM), small batch size, QTC, Kaizen system, cellular layout, standard operating procedures (SOPs), factory-focused, supplier improvement and management, teamwork, visual management and control, etc., were studied with varying degrees of importance for an environment where MSMEs can successfully apply lean.

According to research conducted across Indian MSMEs, the Kanban system was identified as the key lean practice for successful lean implementation in various Indian MSMEs. VSM, Kanban, 5S, TPM, SMED, and Poka-yoke, or mistake proofing, can be applied effectively to reduce system waste and improve productivity (Marasini et al., 2014). The database and information collected during the study, along with the subsequent statistical evaluation performed, indicated that the key and broadly implemented lean techniques were continuous improvement, organisation in the workplace, and standard practices in Indian MSMEs. The SME manufacturers also conducted an exploratory factor analysis to identify the most important lean factors. The factors related to lean that were identified included layout redesign, process optimisation, and work organisation. A set of nine basic lean practices were identified as fundamental elements for lean implementation, affecting the firm's overall performance regardless of its number of processes and size. These methods focused on identifying and eliminating deadly waste in processes. Table 1 describes the goals of various lean tools.

Lean tools and their objectives

Lean Practice	Objective
Pull System	Produce as per the quantity demand
Heijunka	Production leveling
Kaizen	Improve productivity, reduce costs, eliminate unnecessary hard work, and humanize the workplace.
TPM	To maximize the lifespan and productivity of the equipment.

VSM	The information and material flow to increase the visibility of the system
JIT	To reduce inventory holding costs and increase inventory turnover.
Cellular Layout	To increase the productivity with minimizing the cost
Poka-Yoke	Mistake prevention to prevent defects
Takt Time	Synchronize production with demand
5S	Organization at workplace
KANBAN	Identify of potential bottlenecks and fix them so work can flow through them cost-effectively at an optimal speed
Line Balancing	Minimization of idle time to the man of machine
SMED	To reduce set-up time

Table 3.1: Lean Tools and Their Objectives

Improper selection of various lean tools and lack of execution techniques were cited as significant hindrances in implementing lean philosophy in small- and medium-sized enterprises. It is very much clear from the study that different lean practices were recommended and feasible in other manufacturing environments, but many of the lean management practices mentioned were overlapping and unclear. A detailed study was recently done to identify different lean factors and their related lean variables feasible in the various automotive and transactional business environments. The following table describes different lean factors along with their associated lean variables for Indian SMEs in the automotive sector, which provides the foundation for a comprehensive evaluation of the leanness of these SMEs.

3.3. *Lean Measurement System*

A slack-based lean measurement framework based on linear programming was developed with evaluation criteria to measure the extent of efficiency, often known as the lean score. Lean scores measure the importance of various lean practices, quantifying how much value is added and waste reduced (Wan & Chen, 2008). A lean evaluation model, created using fuzzy analytical set theory, is stood up on five essential lean parameters for the Indian auto manufacturing industry.

A fuzzy logic-based theoretical lean measurement system comprised three levels: lean facilitator, lean criteria, and lean attribute, followed by gap assessment. They identified the weak lean criteria, which helped them execute corrective measures to enhance the efficiency of the organization (Vimal & Vinodh, 2012). A mathematical model was created to evaluate how effectively different lean strategies reduce waste in a manufacturing company. This model helped identify a suitable lean strategy for manufacturing organizations. The survey-based approach was used to evaluate the operational efficiency of manufacturing organizations spread across all four geographic boundaries in India that have adopted lean principles and practices. Nearly 80 percent of the organizations adopted lean practices including customer focus, Just In Time production, SMED, statistical process control (SPC), TPM, and collaborative problem-solving. Implementing these lean practices improved productivity and reduced process lead time, inventory accumulated, and space requirements (Ghosh, 2012). An advisory system based on fuzzy logic was formulated to assist SMEs in making decisions regarding lean implementation. This system aims to measure the organization's readiness for lean practices.

Lean factors and associated variables

Extracted factors and labeling	**Explanation of associated variables**
L_1 Identifying and Preventing Problems	l_{11} (Improve the process consistently to stop the flow from occurring)
	l_{12} (After the designing of the product, determine)
	l_{13} (Error proofing to stop problems before they spread extent through the value chain)
	l_{14} (A cause-and-effect diagram can be used to determine the issues underlying causes)
	l_{15} (Standard operating procedure; SOP)
	l_{16} (Statistical process control can be used to overcome the variance)
	l_{17} (Use visual indicators to indicate the problem)
L_2 Strategic partnership with the vendors	l_{21} (Maintain a healthy relationship with our vendors)
	l_{22} (Vendors regularly visit our plant)
	l_{23} (Plant owners visit vendors' plants frequently)
	l_{24} (Maintaining a long-term relationship with our vendors)
	l_{25} (Vendors managed and monitor inventory system)
	l_{26} (Vendors participation in critical product and process design)
	l_{31} (On time raw material review by vendors)

L_3 Production System operates on a pull basis	l_{32} (Production is driven basis on demand at the following station)
	l_{33} (Kanban control system used to oversee inventory in the system)
	l_{34} (Do not accumulate stock in expectation of future demand)
	l_{35} (Customer withdraws the product from the value chain)
L_4 Production flow	l_{41} (Create a group of components that share similar production needs)
	l_{42} (Use production load leveling to sustain the flow of production)
	l_{43} (Develop a set of parts that share comparable routing requirements)
	l_{44} (Equipment is categorized based on the processing requirements of the specific part family)
	l_{45} (Cellular layout for handling a group of specific part)
L_5 Quick Changeover	l_{51} (Employees train regularly to reduce transition time)
	l_{52} (Continuously enhancing the design of our equipment to minimize set up time)
	l_{53} (Continuously work on shortest lead time)
	l_{54} (Align our production cycle time with the customer requirement)
L_6 TPM	l_{61} (Use maintenance activities to enhance productivity)
	l_{62} (enhance the equipment availability through periodic maintenance)
	l_{63} (Provide adequate training to well connect with operators and maintenance staff)
	l_{64} (Implement standard maintenance practices to maintain equipment in optimal condition)
L_7 Engagement of customer	l_{71} (Receive consistent inputs on the quality of the product)
	l_{72} (engagement of customer in product and process design)
	l_{73} (Maintain a healthy and a long-term relationship with customers)

Table 3.2: Lean Factors and Associated Variables

The lean model that considers the various lean principles and practices was developed earlier. The extent of lean readiness directly impacts the resource requirements and plays a crucial role in the outcome of a lean implementation program. A lean assessment system was implemented to continuously evaluate the execution of lean principles using the effectiveness criteria used in manufacturing organizations. The reasoning behind the development of the lean model was an in-depth understanding of the lean implementation change process, which led to alleviating uncertainty and vagueness in lean implementation. The model offered important insights into how including or excluding a specific lean tool could impact leanness and, consequently, the company's operational performance. A structure for creating the cost-effectiveness of various lean tools was evaluated, applying multi-criteria decision-making. The structure was designed with the assistance of the Deming & Kaizen cycle. The QFD (Quality Function Deployment), VSM, and a balanced scorecard were utilized to measure the cost-effectiveness of lean tools concerning customer needs and the challenges related to implementation.

3.4. Lean Measurement Model

A multi-level lean measurement model using a fuzzy comprehensive analysis was suggested to develop a holistic lean measurement system for MSMEs in India's automotive and non-automotive sectors (Chang, 1996). The fundamental idea of the model is that the entire issue can be classified into three levels of hierarchy: level 1 (the top level), level 2 (middle), and level 3 (the bottom one). The average elements at each level of the hierarchy independently operate, especially at the lower level. The assumption also serves as a limitation of the model, facilitating one-way communication flowing from top to bottom.

The below are the step-by-step approaches for creating models:

- Step 1: Set a goal and identify the subject:
  The goal is to achieve a sustainable strategic edge for Indian MSMEs in the automotive sector by adopting lean philosophy.
- Step 2: To evaluate leanness, determine the evaluation score:
  Evaluation grade (set V) = (V1 Excellent, V2 Very Good, V3 Good, V4 Moderate, V5 Poor)
- Step 3: Identification of different lean elements:
  The next significant step in developing a lean measurement model is to define various factors that explain the efficient operations of Indian SMEs in the automotive sector.

$$L = \{L1, L2, L3, L4, L5, L6, L7\}$$

Where F is the lean performance

- Step 4: Identification of different lean subfactors

Lean sub-factors are associated with lean variables to factors.

$L = \{l11, l12, l13, l14, l15, l16\}$
$L = \{l21, l22, l23, l24, l25, l26\}$
$L = \{l31, l32, l33, l34, l35\}$
$L = \{l41, l42, l43, l44, l45\}$
$L = \{l51, l52, l53, l54\}$
$L = \{l61, l62, l63, l64\}$
$L = \{l71, l72, l73\}$

- Step 5: Allocating weight to various factors and their corresponding subfactors using fuzzy AHP

AHP is a highly productive tool for managing the fuzziness present in data. The qualitative evaluation made available by experts is mapped to fuzzy triangular numbers (Table 4), which are used to form a fuzzy pairwise comparison matrix (shown in Table 5). The model consists of three levels: level 1 (Goal), level 2 (Factors), and level 3 (Sub-factors) (refer to Table 5).

- Step 6: Describe the fuzzy membership matrices for each factor. Create a fuzzy membership matrix for every factor and its ln sub-factors.

  Si represents the fuzzy evaluation matrix of factor Li, and sijk indicates the degree of the kth kind of evaluation for factor Li at evaluation level j, which is tied to the factor lij.

- Step 7: For each variable, construct a fuzzy assessment matrix (Judgment Vector). Create a fuzzy assessment matrix for each element using the associated sub-factor weights (level 2) from the fuzzy Analytical Hierarchy Process, where xi = (x1, x2, x3, ______,xn).

  Ai = (Xi × Si) = (ai1, ai2, ______________, aim)

  The fuzzy membership vector Ai signifies how the comment is set to factor Li.

- Step 8: Conduct a fuzzy comprehensive analysis and derive an overall fuzzy membership matrix for the whole system.

$$S = \begin{bmatrix} A1 \\ A2 \\ : \\ : \\ Ai \end{bmatrix} = \begin{bmatrix} a11 & a12 & : & : & a1m \\ a21 & a22 & : & : & a2m \\ : & : & : & : & : \\ : & : & : & : & : \\ an1 & an2 & : & : & anm \end{bmatrix}$$

Suppose the weights calculated for all the factors using fuzzy AHP is represented as X = (X1, X2, – – – – – – – –, Xn).
The overall a comprehensive fuzzy evaluation matrix vector for the complete index system can be represented as A = X × S = (a1, a2, – – – – —, am)

A denotes the mapping of the set of the comments and the entire index system. Let a_0 equal max (a1, a2, ———, am) which is associated with the set of comments i.e. U_k, then U_k represents the assessment of the entire system.
Random Index

N	1.0	2.0	3.0	4.0	5.0	6.0	7.0	8.0	9.0	10.0	11.0
RI	0	0	0.58	0.9	1.11	1.23	1.31	1.42	1.44	1.47	1.52

Table 3.3: RI – (Random Index)

3.5. Suggested Fuzzy AHP Model

3.5.1. HP Procedure

- Step 1: Frame a comparison by evaluating pairs using expert's opinions.

$$\begin{bmatrix} M_{11} & M_{12} & : & : & M_{1n} \\ M_{21} & M_{22} & : & : & M_{2n} \\ : & : & : & : & : \\ : & : & : & : & : \\ M_{n1} & M_{n2} & : & : & M_{nn} \end{bmatrix} \text{-- (1)}$$

- Step 2: Using the given formula to integrate the triangular fuzzy number.

$$N_{ij} = (N_{ij}^{1} \times N_{ij}^{2} \times \_\_\_\_\_\_ \times N_{ij}^{n})^{1/n} \text{ -- (2)}$$

- Step 3: Conduct a consistency to check the decision making process.

Consistency value CU(n) = (CI(n))/RI ≤ 0.1, whereas the consistency index J(n) = (λMax - n)/(n - 1). **λ** Maximum is the greatest eigenvalue of the pair-wise comparison matrix, and n stands for the order of the given matrix. RI is the random index, and its value can be generated with the help of the following table (Table 3). RI is the mean value of CI. The table was framed using the Saaty scale designated by T. L. Saaty, applying simulation through 100 runs.

- Step 4: Calculate the grade consolidation using the following equation.

$$G_i = \sum_{j=1}^{m} N_{ij} \left[\sum_{i=1}^{n} \sum_{j=1}^{m} N_{ij}\right]^{-1} \text{--} (3)$$

- Step 5: Using the following equation, evaluate the consolidated triangular fuzzy number and access the following level of consolidation.

$$U(G_i \geq G_j) = \begin{Bmatrix} 1 & if & m_i \geq m_j \\ 0 & if & l_j \geq u_i \\ \langle l_j - u_j \rangle \div \langle m_i - u_j \rangle - \langle m_j - l_j \rangle & Otherwise \end{Bmatrix} \text{--------} (4)$$

- Step 6: Determine the minimum level of consolidation grade

Min U (G ≥ G_1, G_2, ------- G_k)------------- (5)

Min U ⟨ (G ≥ G_1) and (G ≥ G_2) ---------- and (G ≥ G_k) ⟩

Suppose W_i = Min U ($G_i \geq G_j$) where i = k.

The weight vector can be expressed as X = Normalize the weight vector to obtain the final priority vector.

3.5.2. Triangular Membership Function

A group of five lean specialists was selected for the current study to assess their preferences using the following membership function. The triangular membership function was developed based on fuzzy set theory. These functions were applied for pair-wise comparison. The specialists' subjective evaluations, expressed in linguistic terms, were mapped to their respective fuzzy values (Table 4).

$Nx = (l, m, n) \Rightarrow 1/Nx = (1/l, 1/m, 1/n)$

Triangular fuzzy transformation scale

Linguistic term	The Function (l, m, n)
Equally preferred	(1,1,1), (1,1,2)
Somewhat preferred	(1,2,3), (2,3,4)
Strongly preferred	(3,4,5), (4,5,6)
Highly preferred	(5,6,7), (6,7,8)
Extremely favored	(7,8,9)

Table 3.4: Triangular Fuzzy Transformation Scale

N_{ij}^{k} represents the subjective significance of the ith criterion compared to the jth criterion by the kth expert utilizing the membership function. The below equation determines the value of N_{ij}.

$$N_{ij} = (N_{ij}^{1} \times N_{ij}^{2} \times \_\_\_\_\_\_ \times N_{ij}^{n})^{1/n}$$

Where n represents the no. of experts participating in the decision-making.

3.6. Data Analysis

3.6.1. Weight Indexing

Weight assignment for *L* = (*L1, L2, L3, L4, L5, L6, L7*), Where *L* = Lean performance (Outcomes in value terms) measurement using a fuzzy AHP techniques.

Matrix – A pair wise comparison (value)

	L1	L2	L3	L4	L5	L6	L7
L1	[1 1 1]	4.0 5 6 4.0 5 6 4.0 5 6 3 4.0 5 5 6 7	1.0 1.0 2 1.0 1.0 2 1.0 1.0 2 1.0 1.0 1 1.0 1.0 2	1.0 2 3 1.0 2 3 1.0 2 3 1.0 2 3 1.0 1.0 2	1.0 2 3 1.0 2 3 1.0 1.0 2 1.0 1.0 2 1.0 2 3	1.0 1.0 1.0 1.0 1.0 1.0 1.0 1.0 1.0 1.0 1.0 1.0 1.0 1.0 2	1.0 1.0 1.0 1.0 1.0 0.50 1.0 1.0 1.0 1.0 1.0 0.50 1.0 1.0 1.0
L2	0.25 0.20 0.16 0.25 0.20 0.16 0.25 0.20 0.16 0.33 0.25 0.20 0.20 0.16 0.14	[1 1 1]	0.50 0.33 0.33 0.50 0.33 0.25 0.50 0.33 0.25 0.33 0.25 0.20 0.33 0.25 0.20	1 0.50 0.33 1 0.50 0.33 0.50 0.33 0.25 1 0.50 0.33 0.50 0.33 0.25	0.50 0.33 0.25 0.50 0.33 0.25 1 0.50 3 0.50 0.33 0.25 0.50 0.33 0.25	0.20 0.16 0.14 0.20 0.16 0.14 0.33 0.25 0.20 0.33 025 0.20 033 025 0.20	0.20 0.16 0.14 0.20 0.16 0.14 0.20 0.16 0.14 0.16 0.14 0.12 0.16 0.14 0.12
L3	1.0 1.0 0.50 1.0 1.0 0.50 1.0 1.0 0.50 1.0 1.0 1.0 1.0 1.0 0.50	2.0 3 4.0 2.0 3 4.0 2.0 3 4.0 3 4.0 5 3 4.0 5	[1 1 1]	1.0 2 3 1.0 2 3 1.0 2 3 1.0 1.0 2 1.0 1.0 2	1.0 1.0 2 1.0 1.0 2 1.0 2 3 1.0 1.0 2 1.0 1.0 1.0	1.0 0.50 0.33 1.0 1.0 1.0 1.0 1.0 1.0 1.0 1.0 0.50 1.0 1.0 0.50	1.0 0.50 0.33 1.0 0.50 0.33 1.0 0.50 0.33 1.0 1.0 0.50 1.0 1.0 1.0
L4	1.0 0.50 0.33 1.0 0.50 0.33 1.0 0.50 0.33 1.0 050 0.33 1.0 1.0 0.50	1.0 2.0 3 1.0 2.0 3 2.0 3 4.0 1.0 2.0 3 2.0 3 4.0	1.0 0.50 0.33 1.0 0.50 0.33 1.0 0.50 0.33 1.0 1.0 0.50 1.0 1.0 1.0	[1 1 1]	1.0 1.0 1.0 1.0 1.0 0.50 1.0 1.0 0.50 1.0 0.50 0.33 1.0 1.0 1.0	1.0 0.50 0.33 1.0 0.50 0.33 1.0 0.50 0.33 1.0 0.50 0.33 1.0 1.0 0.50	0.50 0.33 0.25 0.50 0.33 0.25 0.50 0.33 0.25 1.0 0.50 0.33 1.0 0.50 0.33
L5	1.0 0.50 0.33 1.0 0.50 0.33 1.0 1.0 0.50 1.0 1.0 0.50 1.0 0.50 0.33	2.0 3 4.0 2.0 3 4.0 1.0 2 3 2.0 3 4.0 2.0 3 4.0	1.0 1.0 0.50 1.0 0.50 0.33 1.0 1.0 0.50 1.0 1.0 0.50 1.0 1.0 1.0	1.0 1.0 1 1.0 1.0 2 1.0 1.0 2 1.0 2 3 1.0 1.0 1.0	[1 1 1]	1.0 0.50 0.33 1.0 0.50 0.33 1.0 0.50 0.33 1.0 0.50 0.33 1.0 1.0 1.0	1.0 0.50 0.33 1.0 0.50 0.33 1.0 0.50 0.33 1.0 0.50 0.33 1.0 1.0 0.50
L6	1.0 1.0 1.0 1.0 1.0 1.0 1.0 1.0 1.0 1.0 1.0 1.0 1.0 1.0 0.50	5.0 6 7 5 6 7 3.0 4.0 5 3.0 4.0 5 3.0 4.0 5	1.0 2 3 1.0 1.0 1.0 1.0 1.0 1.0 1.0 1.0 2 1.0 1.0 2	1.0 2 3 1.0 2 3 1.0 2 3 1.0 2 3 1.0 1.0 2	1.0 2 3 1.0 2 3 1.0 2 3 1.0 2 3 1.0 1.0 1.0	[1 1 1]	1.0 1.0 0.50 1.0 1.0 0.50 1.0 1.0 0.50 1.0 1.0 0.50 1.0 1.0 1.0
L7	1.0 1.0 1.0 1.0 1.0 2 1.0 1.0 1.0 1.0 1.0 2 1.0 1.0 1.0	5.0 6 7 5.0 6 7 5.0 6 7 6.0 7 8 66.0 7 8	1.0 2 3 1.0 2 3 1.0 2 3 1.0 1.0 2 1.0 1.0 1.0	2 3 4.0 2 3 4.0 2 3 4.0 1.0 2 4.0 1.0 2 3	1.0 2 3 1.0 2 3 1.0 2 3 1.0 2 3 1.0 1.0 2	1.0 1.0 1.0 1.0 1.0 2 1.0 1.0 2 1.0 1.0 2 1.0 1.0 1.0	[1 1 1]

Table 3.5: Matrix –A Pair Wise Comparison (Value)

A group of five lean specialists was formed. Lean specialists are consultants with at least four to five years of expertise in implementing lean in Indian SMEs.

- Step 1: Perform a pair-wise comparison and convert the experts' opinions into fuzzy triangular numbers (Table 5).
- Step 2: Perform a consistency evaluation of the pairwise comparison matrix.

The max. evaluation of the pairwise comparison matrix is 7.36.

$GI(n) = \frac{\lambda Max - n}{n-1}$, n = 7 GI(n) = 0.06

Value of SI = 1.32

Consistency value

$GU(n) = \frac{CI(n)}{RI}$ = GU(n) = 0.045

The consistency value falls below 0.1, which means it can be safely concluded that the expert's decision taken in creating of the pairwise comparison matrix is consistent.

- Step 3: By executing the equation (3) to the consolidation of the triangular fuzzy numbers, we get the below set of values:

G_1 = (0.120, 0.179, 0.30),
G_2 = (0.025, 0.05, 0.069),
G_3 = (0.089, 0.15, 0.079),
G_4 = (0.059, 0.110, 0.10),
G_5 = (0.061, 0.121, 0.20),
G_6 = (0.110, 0.190, 0.29),
G_7 = (0.141, 0.231, 0.39)

- Step 4: Using equations 4 & 5, calculate the following grade.

Min U ($G_1 \geq G_2, G_3, G_4, G_5, G_6, G_7$) = *0.78,*
Min U ($G_2 \geq G_1, G_3, G_4, G_5, G_6, G_7$) = *0.12,*
Min U ($G_3 \geq G_1, G_2, G_4, G_5, G_6, G_7$) = *0.49,*
Min U ($G_4 \geq G_1, G_2, G_3, G_5, G_6, G_7$) = *0.19,*
Min U ($G_5 \geq G_1, G_2, G_3, G_4, G_6, G_7$) = *0.34,*
Min U ($G_6 \geq G_1, G_2, G_3, G_4, G_5, G_7$) = *0.79,*
Min U ($G_7 \geq G_1, G_2, G_3, G_4, G_5, G_6$) = *1.00,*

Obtaining the weight vector = (0.78, 0.12, 0.49, 0.19, 0.34, 0.79, 1), and normalizing this weight vector generates the priority vector, which explains the relative significance of the factors related to the degree of leanness. (L1, L2, L3, L4, L5, L6, L7) = (0, 22, 0.04, 0.13, 0.055, 0.95, 0.22, 0.27). Similarly, the priority vectors for each of the sub-factors classified as level 3 factors can be calculated in relation to their corresponding factors at level 1 using the above-described methodology.

Using the fuzzy AHP approach and methodology, the weight index for the complete measurement system was developed. The table below outlines the weight index for the measurement system (Table 6).

Goal	Level 1: Primary Factor	Weight	level 2: Secondary Factors	Weight
Measurement Of Leanness	L_1 Identifying and Preventing Problems	0.22	l_{11} (Continuous process flow improvement)	0.12
			l_{12} (PCI; the process capacity calculation)	0.16
			l_{13} (Poka-yoke; the mistake proofing)	0.19
			l_{14} (Use the Ishikawa or the fishbone diagram diagram)	0.18
			l_{15} (Standardized operational procedures)	0.12
			l_{16} (Use SPC; to minimize variability)	0.18
			l_{17} (Use visual identifications to identify the issues)	0.06
	L_2 Strategic Partnership with the Vendors	0.04	l_{21} (Maintain a healthy relationship with our vendors)	0.20
			l_{22} (Suppliers regularly visit our plant)	0.07
			l_{23} (Plant owner must visit the facilities of their vendors)	0.06
			l_{24} (Maintaining a long-term and a healthy bound with our vendors)	0.21
			l_{25} (Vendors controlled inventory system)	0.19
			l_{26} (Vendors participation in designing the process and product)	0.24
	L_3 Production System	0.13	l_{31} (On time receive the raw material (RM) by the vendors)	0.11

	Operates on a pull basis		l_{32} (Pull Production process system)	0.26
			l_{33} (Kanban; a ticketing system process/product control)	0.24
			l_{34} (Avoid building inventory for future expectation)	0.22
			l_{35} (Customer must pulls the valuable product from the value chain)	0.14
	L_4 Production Flow	0.055	l_{41} (Create a group of components having similar production need)	0.25
			l_{42} (Use the production load leveling to control and maintain the production flow)	0.11
			l_{43} (Create a group of parts having similar routing specifications)	0.19
			l_{44} (Equipment is categorized according to processing needs of the part family)	0.17
			l_{45} (Cellular layout design for handling a part family)	0.27
	L_5 Quick Changeover	0.095	l_{51} (Employees engage in practice regularly to minimize change over time; COT)	0.39
			l_{52} (A equipment design frequently to minimize set up time)	0.24
			l_{53} (Focus on continuous vendors lead time reduction)	0.16
			l_{54} (Align our production cycle time (CT) with the customer demand)	0.19
	L_6 TPM	0.22	l_{61} (Use maintenance activities as a tool to improve productivity)	0.33
			l_{62} (a cyclical maintenance and check)	0.27
			l_{63} (Autonomous maintenance)	0.21
			l_{64} (Use standardized checks and maintenance procedure)	0.19

	L_7 Engagement of Customer	0.27	l_{71} (Call out for regular feedback regarding the product quality)	0.26
			l_{72} (Customer participations in product and process design)	0.38
			l_{73} (Develop a long-term healthy relationship with our customers)	0.38

Table 3.6: Weight indexing

3.5.2. Fuzzy Comprehensive Analysis

Based on the group of 50 specialists from 50 Indian MSMEs, the study evaluated the current conditions of lean MSMEs in India's automotive and non-automotive sectors. It helped determine how to implement various lean principles and practices. All the specialists were managers in their respective industries and processes. The fuzzy evaluation matrix for factors F1 to F7 is being framed on the basis of the evaluation criteria outlined in the model development section.

For example, when it comes to the f11 and level 3 factor, nine experts rated it as good, 16 as moderate, and 25 as poor. S11 = f11 fuzzy vector (0.1, 0.1, 0.19, 0.31, 0.49). Similarly, the fuzzy vectors for the following are:

S_{12} = (0.0, 0.10, 0.14, 0.36, 0.51),

S_{13} = (0.1, 0.00, 0.11, 0.27, 0.59),

S_{14} = (0.0, 0.1, 0.15, 0.37, 0.49),

S_{15} = (0.0, 0.00, 0.23, 0.36, 0.41),

S_{16} = (0.1, 0.09, 0.15, 0.25, 0.55),

S_{17} = (0.0, 0.11, 0.14, 0.31, 0.32),

The fuzzy evaluation matrix for factor F_1 is as follows:

$$S_1 = \begin{bmatrix} 0.1 & 0.1 & 0.19 & 0.31 & 0.49 \\ 0.0 & 0.1 & 0.14 & 0.36 & 0.51 \\ 0.1 & 0.0 & 0.11 & 0.27 & 0.59 \\ 0.0 & 0.1 & 0.15 & 0.37 & 0.49 \\ 0.0 & 0.0 & 0.23 & 0.36 & 0.41 \\ 0.1 & 0.09 & 0.15 & 0.25 & 0.55 \\ 0.0 & 0.11 & 0.14 & 0.31 & 0.32 \end{bmatrix}$$

The fuzzy assessment matrix for all other factors can be structured similarly:

$$S_2 = \begin{bmatrix} 0.1 & 0.02 & 0.11 & 0.14 & 0.74 \\ 0.1 & 0.01 & 0.14 & 0.23 & 0.59 \\ 0.0 & 0.09 & 0.11 & 0.36 & 0.42 \\ 0.0 & 0.04 & 0.09 & 0.25 & 0.61 \\ 0.1 & 0.0 & 0.0 & 0.21 & 0.79 \\ 0.0 & 0.1 & 0.1 & 0.29 & 0.71 \end{bmatrix}$$

$$S_3 = \begin{bmatrix} 0.1 & 0.2 & 0.02 & 0.39 & 0.59 \\ 0.0 & 0.1 & 0.09 & 0.71 & 0.22 \\ 0.1 & 0.0 & 0.24 & 0.74 & 0.02 \\ 0.0 & 0.0 & 0.14 & 0.64 & 0.21 \\ 0.0 & 0.1 & 0.16 & 0.44 & 0.39 \end{bmatrix}$$

$$S_4 = \begin{bmatrix} 0.1 & 0.0 & 0.02 & 0.20 & 0.80 \\ 0.1 & 0.1 & 0.04 & 0.24 & 0.69 \\ 0.1 & 0.0 & 0.06 & 0.32 & 0.59 \\ 0.0 & 0.2 & 0.09 & 0.44 & 0.44 \\ 0.0 & 0.0 & 0.10 & 0.21 & 0.81 \end{bmatrix}$$

$$S_5 = \begin{bmatrix} 0.1 & 0.0 & 0.11 & 0.81 & 0.11 \\ 0.0 & 0.2 & 0.0 & 0.19 & 0.80 \\ 0.1 & 0.2 & 0.22 & 0.10 & 0.91 \\ 0.1 & 0.1 & 0.21 & 0.59 & 0.21 \end{bmatrix}$$

$$S_6 = \begin{bmatrix} 0.0 & 0.21 & 0.24 & 0.36 & 0.21 \\ 0.1 & 0.25 & 0.26 & 0.44 & 0.04 \\ 0.1 & 0.19 & 0.33 & 0.35 & 0.16 \\ 0.0 & 0.2 & 0.10 & 0.43 & 0.46 \end{bmatrix}$$

$$S_7 = \begin{bmatrix} 0.1 & 0.11 & 0.26 & 0.25 & 0.41 \\ 0.0 & 0.1 & 0.1 & 0.03 & 0.96 \\ 0.1 & 0.10 & 0.60 & 0.32 & 0.2 \end{bmatrix}$$

The weight vectors (Level 3) of secondary factor are shown in Table 5

X_1 = (0.12, 0.16, 0.19, 0.18, 0.12, 0.18, 0.06)

X_2 = (0.20, 0.07, 0.06, 0.21, 0.19, 0.24)

X_3 = (0.11, 0.26, 0.24, 0.22, 0.14)

X_4 = (0.25, 0.11, 0.19, 0.17, 0.27)

X_5 = (0.39, 0.24, 0.16, 0.19)

X_6 = (0.33, 0.27, 0.21, 0.19)

X_7 = (0.26, 0.38, 0.38)

Fuzzy vector associated with factor F1 is A1, (A1= X1 × S1), thus: A1 = (00, 0.024, 0.154, 0.33, 0.49). Similarly, for all other factors:

A_2 = (00, 0.01, 0.05, 0.22, 0.69)

A_3 = (00, 0.00, 0.11, 0.62, 0.22)

A_4 = (00, 0.00, 0.02, 0.26, 0.69)
A_5 = (00, 0.00, 0.07, 0.50, 0.42)
A_6 = (00, 0.16, 0.25, 0.39, 0.20)
A_7 = (00, 0.05, 0.27, 0.18, 0.06)

A fuzzy assessment matrix for the complete measurement system can be well written in the following way:

$$S = \begin{bmatrix} A_1 \\ A_2 \\ A_3 \\ A_4 \\ A_5 \\ A_6 \\ A_7 \end{bmatrix} = \begin{bmatrix} 0.0 & 0.02 & 0.15 & 0.33 & 0.49 \\ 0.0 & 0.01 & 0.05 & 0.22 & 0.69 \\ 0.0 & 0.0 & 0.11 & 0.62 & 0.22 \\ 0.0 & 0.0 & 0.02 & 0.26 & 0.69 \\ 0.0 & 0.0 & 0.07 & 0.50 & 0.42 \\ 0.0 & 0.16 & 0.25 & 0.39 & 0.20 \\ 0.0 & 0.05 & 0.27 & 0.18 & 0.06 \end{bmatrix}$$

Table 7 is used to convert the assessment grade into a numerical score. Categorization of Sustainable Competitive Advantage

Leanness Score	90-100	70-90	60-70	40-60	0-40
Valuation grade (U)	Excellent	Very Good	Good	Moderate	Poor

Table 3.7: Categorization of Sustainable Competitive Advantage

The Evaluation Grade:

U = Excellent, Very Good, Good, Moderate, Poor; 95, 80, 65, 50, 20

The cumulative weight vector for the measurement system is X = (0.22, 0.04, 0.13, 0.055, 0.095, 0.22, 0.27). The fuzzy vector representing the overall measurement system can be framed as:

A = X × S = (0.0, 0.059, 0.177, 0.32, 0.37)

The maximum value of A is 0.37, which linked to the poor (U5) in the comment set. This clearly indicates that the status of lean in Indian MSMEs is somehow lacking, reflected by the calculated value of A × U= 39.33. Similarly, the numerical score of the evaluation of factors L1 to L7 is (38.074, 30.57, 43.77, 29.93, 38.29, 53.03, 33.81).

3.7. Hypothesis Testing

3.7.1. Implementation of Lean Helps SMEs to Transform Business and Operational Process

The above Lean Measurement System (LMS) – Model was evaluated using Structural Equation Modeling (SEM) in LISREL (Linear Structural Relation) version 8.8. The t-values of the variable vary between 3.04 and 5.86, which is well within the range of expected levels at the significance level of 0.05; the findings of the hypothesis have been organized in Table 10.

LMS (Lean Measurement System) Path	Hypothesis	Estimated Point	T-Value	Hypothesis Support
Effective Leadership	H1	0.94	4.87	Yes
Organizational Culture Change	H2	1.02	5.40	Yes
Employee Involvement	H3	0.84	4.26	Yes
Willingness to acquire knowledge	H4	0.79	3.34	Yes
Corporate financial Capabilities	H5	1.08	5.86	Yes
Leadership Commitment	H6	1.03	5.46	Yes
Continual Evaluation	H7	0.96	5.00	Yes
Education and Training	H8	0.90	4.60	Yes
Sharing of knowledge	H9	0.99	5.12	Yes
Initiatives to business strategies	H10	1.01	5.30	Yes
Facilitator	H11	0.80	4.02	Yes

Table 3.8: Testing of Hypothesis

The factors identified by the SME model are considered for the relative weighting and importance of the criteria. The relative weighting of the criteria has been determined and is presented in Table 11.

Importance of the critical elements

Effective Leadership	Change in Organizational	Employee Involvement	Willingness to learn	Company Financial Capabilities	Commitment of Top Management	Continual Evaluation	Comprehensive Education and	Knowledge Sharing	Initiatives to business strategies	Facilitator
0.099	0.178	0.089	0.836	0.114	0.108	0.102	0.094	0.104	0.106	0.084

Table 3.9: Importance of the Critical Elements

3.7.1.1. AHP Process

In this approach and method,

- The collected information is broken down into a structured arrangement of alternatives and criteria.
- The information is then synchronized to determine the comparative ranking of alternatives.
- The information judgement can be used to compare qualitative and quantitative data to derive their weight and priorities.
- Goal:
- Select the best options.
- Set a priority for options.
- List the set criteria.

Procedure

Step – 1: Prioritize the criteria.

Step – 2: Rank options based on each criterion.

Step – 3: Standardize the ranking of options.

Numerical Value	Verbal Scale	Explanation
1.0	Given the equal significance of both the components	Two components contribute equally
3.0	The importance of one element is moderately greater than another	The experience and judgment support one element more than the other.
5.0	A strongly emphasis of one element compared to other	An element is highly preferred

7.0	The critical importance of one element compared to another	An element is extremely dominant.
9.0	The critical importance of one element over another	A certain element is favoured by at least a factor of ten
2.0, 4.0, 6.0, 8.0	Intermediate values	Used to compromise between two different opinions

Table 3.10: Thomas L. Saaty's Scale: A Pair Wise Comparison Matrix

Pair wise comparison matrix is explained above in table 12.
Step – 1: Pair wise comparison matrix of alternatives.

	G1	**G2**	**G3**	**G4**	**G5**	**G6**
G1	1	3	2	6	5	5
G2		1	3	5	3	1
G3			1	3	1	0.32
G4				1	0.24	0.21
G5					1	0.34
G6						1

Table 3.11: Pair Wise Comparison Matrix of Alternatives

Pair-wise comparisons matrix of alternatives is explained in Table 13. After this, we obtain the relative weight value for each alternative and conclude with the weightage in Table 14.

Maximum eigen value = 6.4573 C. I. = 0.09147 Weights (Eigen Vector)	
0.4180	G1
0.1887	G2
0.0955	G3
0.0358	G4
0.0816	G5
0.1801	G6
1.0000	Total

Table 3.12: Relative Weights of the Alternatives

Step – 2: Pair wise comparison matrix in terms of organization structure.

	G1	G2	G3	G4	G5	G6
G1	1	0.033	0.5	0.249	0.16	0.24
G2		1	0.33	0.249	0.24	0.5
G3			1	0.51	0.24	0.33
G4				1	1	2
G5					1	3
G6						1

Table 3.13; Pair Wise Comparison Matrix in Terms of Organization Structure

A pairwise comparison matrix is made by pairing all the MSMEs against one another is given in Table 15.

Maximum eigen value = 6.3407 **C. I. = 0.0681** **Weights (Eigen Vector)**	
0.0458	C1
0.0765	C2
0.1108	C3
0.2599	C4
0.3362	C5
0.1705	C6
1.0000	Total

Table 3.14: Relative Weights for Alternatives Based on Organization

The alternative weightage obtained for alternatives based on organizational structure is given in Table 16. The relative importance of the fifth MSME is higher, whereas the weight attributed to the first MSME is the lowest of the six.

After obtaining the relative weights for alternatives based on organizational structure, repeat the same procedure for all criteria, and thus we get the result shown below in Table 17.

AHP Results						
	C1	**C2**	**C3**	**C4**	**C5**	**C6**
Effective Leadership	0.418056	0.188783	0.095509	0.035861	0.081641	0.18015
Change in Organizational Culture	0.045802	0.076525	0.110862	0.259969	0.336282	0.17056

Employee Involvement	0.033818	0.057967	0.111582	0.298939	0.300323	0.197371
Willingness to learn	0.420986	0.192683	0.073422	0.036824	0.092371	0.183714
Company Financial Capabilities	0.404035	0.225296	0.071806	0.039213	0.086785	0.172865
Commitment of Top Management	0.317361	0.185776	0.057455	0.075187	0.154169	0.210053
Continual Evaluation	0.418056	0.188783	0.095509	0.035861	0.081641	0.18015
Comprehensive Education and Training	0.424713	0.191349	0.077909	0.036774	0.077909	0.191349
Knowledge Sharing	0.367053	0.161424	0.085058	0.090517	0.105406	0.190543
Initiatives to business strategies	0.404035	0.225296	0.071806	0.039213	0.086785	0.172865
Facilitator	0.106217	0.106217	0.286507	0.181334	0.227457	0.092269
Total	3.360132	1.800099	1.137425	1.129692	1.630769	1.941889

Table 3.15: AHP Results

The results are formulated after performing the analytical hierarchy process on six MSMEs' eleven critical success factors. The different critical factors are tabulated, and importance is given to each by the six MSMEs.

3.7.1.2. Results

Lean manufacturing is a widespread and comprehensive manufacturing approach and methodology that is focused on optimizing capacity and minimizing system variability. The factor provided by the SEM model is considered to determine the relative significance of the given criteria. The relative criteria are based on LISREL and are explained in Table 18.

Weight Ages of the Essential Factor

Sr. No.	Critical Success Factors	Weight
1	Effective Leadership	0.099
2	Change in Organizational Culture	0.107
3	Employee Involvement	0.089
4	Willingness to learn	0.083

5	Company Financial Capabilities	0.114
6	Commitment of Top Management	0.108
7	Continual Evaluation	0.102
8	Comprehensive Education and Training	0.094
9	Knowledge Sharing	0.104
10	Initiatives to business strategies	0.106
11	Facilitator	0.084

Table 3.16: Weight Ages of the Essential Factor

The table above presents the relative weight attributed to all the eleven success factors, indicating that the financial capabilities turned out to be the topmost priority of the industries.

MSMEs	Rank
G1	1
G2	3
G3	5
G4	6
G5	4
G6	2

Table 3.17: AHP Ranking

Using AHP procedures will enhance the support for our findings. The ranking offered by these methods indicates a more effective application of the lean measurement techniques in C1 industries.

Thus, implementing the lean approach in the MSMEs in India mainly focused on minimizing wastage. This waste results in an excess of working capital, which in turn negatively impacts the organization's monetary advantage. Identifying and prioritizing the critical factors influencing the implementation of lean in the MSME sector is a multi-criteria decision-making challenge. This problem has been addressed using Structural Equation Modelling (SEM). The monetary impact regarding all eleven critical factors proved to be valid in the causal analysis. The ranking obtained from the AHP model provides valuable guidance for organizations to focus on various important factors while working towards their targets. This model facilitates the execution of lean principles in MSMEs in India.

3.7.8. The MSME Sector Exports Outperformed the Total Exports from India, and the Share of Exports Has Also Increased

3.7.8.1. The MSME sector exports outperformed the total exports from India

- Step – 1: Draft or hypothesis.

H_0: The MSME sector export has no significant performance of the total exports from India.

H_1: The MSME sector export has a significant performance of the total exports from India.

$\alpha = 0.05$

$H_0: \beta_1 = 0$

$H_1: \beta_1 \neq 0$

- Step – 2: Drawing Simple linear regression (SLR)

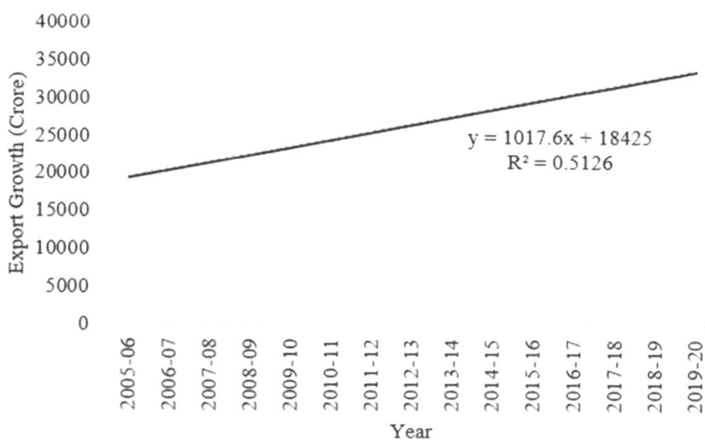

Figure 3.1: Simple Linear Regression

- Step – 3: Analysis of Variance (AV)

Regression Statistics	
Multiple R	0.838
R Square	0.702
Adjusted R Square	0.677
Standard Error	30.470
Observations	14

ANOVA

	df	*SS*	*MS*	*F*	*Significance F*
Regression	1	266856075.92	266856075.9	28.21327697	0.018480515
Residual	12	113502338.44	9458528.203		
Total	13	380358414.36			

	Coefficients	*Standard Error*	*t Stat*	*P-value*	*Lower 95%*	*Upper 95%*	*Lower 95.0%*	*Upper 95.0%*
Intercept	6900.271051	3965.346645	1.740143213	0.107390538	-1739.477094	15540.0192	-1739.477094	15540.0192
D - Test Score	2	0.091290239	5.311617171	0.018480515	0.285994456	0.683803143	0.285994456	0.683803143

Table 3.18: Analysis of Variance

Result:

P-value = 0.018 is less than α = 0.05; thus, we shall reject H0 (null hypothesis) and accept H1 (alternative hypothesis), as there is sufficient evidence to reject H0; therefore, it has been proved that the MSME sector's exports significantly outperformed the total exports from India in the post-liberalization period (2005–2020).

3.7.8.2. The Share of MSME Exports Has Increased After the Economic Reforms

Step – 1: Draft or hypothesis.

H_0: The share of MSME export has not increased.

H_1: The share of MSME export has increased.

$\alpha = 0.05$

H_0: $\beta_1 = 0$

H_1: $\beta_1 \neq 0$

Step – 2: Drawing Simple linear regression (SLR)

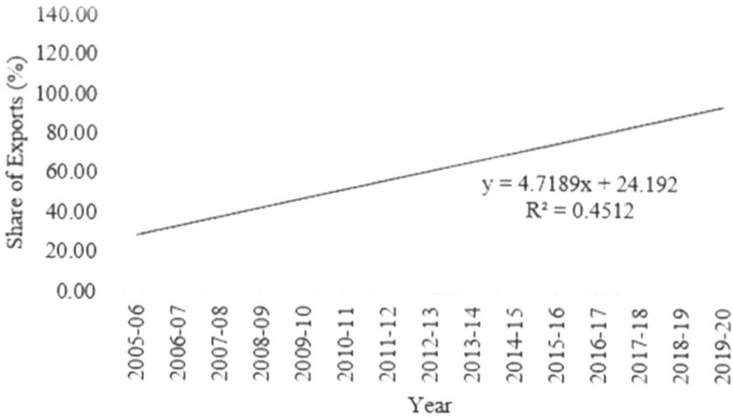

Figure 3.2: Simple Linear Regressions

Step – 3: Analysis of Variance (AV)

Regression Statistics	
Multiple R	0.630478802
R Square	0.39750352
Adjusted R Square	0.34729548
Standard Error	25.29181284
Observations	14

ANOVA

	df	*SS*	*MS*	*F*	*Significance F*
Regression	1	5064.395677	5064.395677	7.917128808	0.015640547
Residual	12	7676.109559	639.6757966		
Total	13	12740.50524			

	Coefficients	*Standard Error*	*t Stat*	*P-value*	*Lower 95%*	*Upper 95%*	*Lower 95.0%*	*Upper 95.0%*
Intercept	13.21677727	19.34177879	0.68332791	0.507379144	-28.92533849	55.35889304	-28.92533849	55.35889304
32.81	0.711321474	0.252802907	2.813739293	0.015640547	0.160511256	1.262131692	0.160511256	1.262131692

Table 3.19: Analysis of Variance

Result:

P-value = 0.015 is less than α = 0.05; thus, we shall reject H0 (null hypothesis) and accept H1 (alternative hypothesis), as there is sufficient evidence to reject H0. Therefore, it has been proved that the share of MSME exports has significantly increased after the economic reforms of the Indian economy.

3.8. Discussion and Conclusion

In a rapid globalization era, organizations around the globe are striving to develop a manufacturing strategy that can provide them with a sustainable competitive advantage. As a result, recognizing the factors that drive long-term competitive advantages is crucial. The key driver is the judicious application of various lean practices, which improve resource efficiency and minimize unwanted tasks in the system. However, a more detailed study is required to identify the key lean elements that could boost the efficiency or the lean performance of Indian MSMEs. As a result, they attain significant long-term strategic advantages compared to their competitors. One of the outcomes of the study was the development and establishment of a framework that describes different lean factors and their corresponding sub-factors. These factors act as important key drivers influencing the leanness of the automotive MSME sectors in India for future improvement. A fuzzy AHP methodology was utilized to determine the importance of these factors. Finally, a fuzzy comprehensive analysis was conducted to evaluate the status of leanness in Indian SMEs.

The suggested model employs fuzzy comprehensive analysis to evaluate the level of leanness in Indian MSMEs. The existing leanness in Indian SMEs is inadequate in terms of resource optimization, waste reduction, and engaging customers in process design and product development. Although many SMEs in India, especially in the automotive industries, have started executing different lean principles and practices, they still lack a clear understanding of numerous lean methodologies, their benefits, and potential outcomes in the form of sustainable strategic advantage. The suggested measurement model could be linked to the various lean factors, their elements, potential opportunities, and the possible outcomes. By creating a clear and practical understanding of lean practices, Indian SMEs can effectively, wisely, and fairly incorporate a series of diversified lean methodologies. They must prioritize crucial lean elements and their related sub-factors to gain optimal advantage. As per the numerical evaluation scores, the three most significant factors identified are customer engagement, problem detection and prevention, and TPM. In addition, their numerically evaluated values were 33.81, 38.074, and

53.05 for customer involvement, problem recognition & prevention, and TPM, respectively. These scores suggest the weak and inadequate contribution of the essential factors in promoting leanness, which could provide a significant sustainable strategic benefit to Indian SMEs. The primary focus should be on improving these key elements and associated tasks to gain a substantial and lasting strategic advantage and excel in the competitive global landscape.

Though the suggested model comprehensively defines and quantifies the level of leanness related to sustainable strategic advantage for Indian SMEs, the subjective nature of evaluating real entities cannot be overlooked. The factors related to agility ought to be incorporated into the model to evaluate an organization's ability to respond in an increasingly unpredictable and challenging business environment. By incorporating criteria for both leanness and agility, we can establish reliable measures for the sustainable strategic advantage of Indian automotive SMEs.

Further to the study, it has also been observed that the performance of India's MSMEs towards the contribution to India's exports with the help of lean methodology has increased over the period. All the hypotheses have been proven through the structural equation modeling of lean practices. It is worth mentioning that the performance of small and medium-sized enterprises (SMEs) is positively correlated with personal, business, and technical skills.

Chapter 4| Development of an Integrated Lean Practice Model

4.1. Introduction

The performance of any organization is determined by how effectively its resources are utilized. The lean manufacturing approach and methodology is a technique used to enhance the efficiency of an organization by eliminating or minimizing its waste. Many industries make extensive use of lean manufacturing tools and techniques. The performance of an organization is evaluated through key performance indicators, which normally include the rate of production, quality, availability of a machine, cycle time (CT), rejection rate, and utilization of resources. Various tools and techniques are available in the market to evaluate lean implementation, but scientific approaches for selecting lean tools are rarely found in the literature. Therefore, this chapter introduces a comprehensive model that integrates FMEA, Analytic Hierarchy Process (AHP), and QFD under a fuzzy context.

The proposed method is formulated in phases by addressing the problems identified by reviewers and specialists from different organizations. This approach and methodology are outlined in three different models. The first model integrates VSM, plant layout, FQFD, and FFMEA to identify the key resources responsible for generating major wastes in the organization. The second model incorporates only FFMEA along with VSM and the layout of the plant to address the limitations of the first model. Later, the third model employs FAHP and FQFD to address the shortcomings of the second model. Case studies from three different organizations have clearly shown the effectiveness of the developed model.

4.1.1. Model 1: VSM Plant Layout – FQFD – FFMEA Integrated Model

The proposed model shown in figure 3.1 integrates VSM, the layout of the plant, FQFD, and FFMEA. The model is developed by integrating two techniques, FQFD and FFMEA, to achieve the purpose of LT selection. The main purpose is to target the critical resources called personnel, equipment, material, and schedule (Sawhney, R., et al.,

2010), which lead to the generation of waste. The subsequent sections provide a detailed, step-by-step procedure for constructing this model.

4.1.1.1. Stage 1: Creating a Visual Representation of the Plant Layout and Formulating a Current State VSM

Value stream mapping (VSM) is an operational flow management technique developed from lean manufacturing for analyzing, designing, and managing the material and information flow required to deliver a product to a customer. It is also characterized as "material and information-flow mapping." It depicts various work streams and information flows using a system of standard symbols. Items are mapped as adding or not adding value from the customer's standpoint to root out items that do not add value. The initial phase of this model is plotting the existing plant layout and formulating the current state VSM by closely monitoring production activities and gathering information about production processes. The current state VSM and the plant layout are then reviewed and redesigned. The plant layout is created to scale to estimate transportation and motion distances and space utilization. Both the VSM and the plant layout show the complete view of how men, material, equipment, and information flow throughout the process. This enables the plant manager to decide whether the current system should be maintained or changed. If the ongoing system is not satisfactory, stage 2 will be executed.

4.1.1.2. Stage 2: Waste Identification, Determining Critical Resources, and Ranking Them Using FQFD

In stage 2, waste is recognized through closely observing the current state of VSM and the layout of the plant.

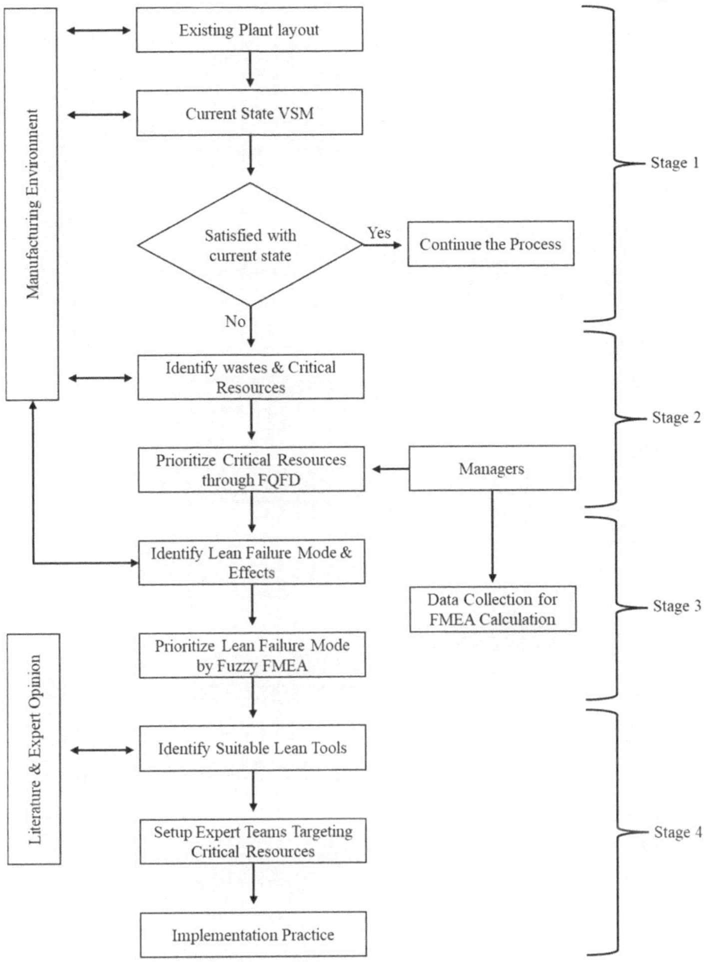

Figure 4.1: VSM Plant Layout – FQFD – FFMEA - Combined Model

The key resources contributing to these wastes are identified based on the conversation among the managers of the organizations. The idea of this phase is to prioritize the vital critical resources. This is achieved by incorporating FQFD and considering the organization's waste and the most critical resources. The identified wastes are found in place of the customer need, and critical resources are related to the functional requirement. The technical and target analysis and planning matrices are not deemed relevant to this study, so they are not included (Almannai et al., 2008). The inputs of the plant managers, supervisors, operations controller, and other specialists in the organization are gathered to assess the correlations and Relative Importance (RI). The relationships between these factors are represented through suggestions using a fuzzy triangular number. To prioritize the identified unwanted activities, Wi (i=1, n) should be given weight and significance. The fuzzy triangular numbers on the four-point linguistic scale that correspond to importance weights are explained in Table 3.1, which illustrates the significant weights for the identified wastes (Bottani E. & Rizzi A., 2006).

Weight (W_i) Importance	Fuzzy Number
Very Heigh (VH)	(0.8, 1, 1)
High (H)	(0.6, 0.8, 1)
Low (L)	(0, 0.4, 0.5)
Extremely Low (EL)	(0, 0.1, 0.4)

Table 4.1: Fuzzy Numbers with Significance Weights for Evaluating Wastes

A suggestion noted as an entry (i,j) in the House of Quality (HoQ) shows the relationship matrix, which indicates the better associations Rij (i = 1,…,n; j = 1,…,m) between the graded wastes and the identified crucial resources. This association represents the strength of the crucial resource 'j' in relation to waste 'i'. The degree of association is also explained in terms of fuzzy triangular numbers. The fuzzy numbers corresponding to the degree of relationships, explained in Table 3.2, are used for this purpose (Bottani & Rizzi, 2006).

Degree of relationship	Fuzzy Number
Strong (S)	(0.8, 1, 1)
Medium (M)	(0.3, 0.4, 0.6)
Weak (W)	(0, 0, 0.4)

Table 4.2: Fuzzy Values for Relationship Matrix

In House of Quality, the relationship intensity to all crucial resources is determined by considering how one resource impacts another in relation to waste effects. The weights are derived from opinions and conducted surveys. The correlation matrix located at the top of the roof of HoQ explains the mutual benefits of one resource RIj on the other RIj′ (j ≠ j′). This relationship is utilized to calculate the final weight of the crucial resources. The fuzzy numbers indicate these correlations, which are assessed on a four-point linguistic scale, varying from "strong positive" to "strong negative," as explained in Table 3.3 (Bottani, 2009).

Degree of correlation (DC)	Fuzzy Number
Very positive (VP)	(0.3, 0.4, 0.6)
Positive (P)	(0, 0.4, 0.5)
Negative (N)	(-0.4, -0.4, 0)
Very Negative (SN)	(-0.6, -0.5, -0.3)

Table 4.3: Degree of Association with Corresponding Fuzzy Numbers

The relatively significance and final score of the jth critical resource are calculated using the following equations (Bottani, 2009):

$RI_j = \sum_{i=1}^{n} W_i \times R_{ij}$ j=1,……,m (1.1)

$Score_j = RI_j \times \sum_{j' \neq j} T_{jj} \times RI_i$ j=1,……,m (1.2)

The final scores obtained from the equation (3.2) are representing fuzzy numbers (l, m, u). to rank the critical resources, it is important to convert the fuzzy score into a specific value. The specific value is determined using the formula shown below (Bottani, 2009):

$Crisp\ Value = \frac{1+2m+u}{4}$ (1.3)

4.1.1.3. Stage 3: Identification and Prioritize Ranking of Lean Failure Mode (LFMs) Using FFMEA Technique

Implementing lean transformations (LTs) for all the critical resources can be expensive and labour-intensive. The organizations may be hesitant to commit to a major change that might take significant time to yield a positive outcome. Thus, organizations should opt for a continual improvement approach for a successful lean transformation. For this, it is very critical to identify a significant resource for targeting. This identification is facilitated by FQFD. By following this, a deep investigation is carried out to understand the causes behind an organization's failure. The elements through which an organization produces waste are termed lean failure modes (LFMs) and are

characterized by the type of waste. The root causes and impacts of LFMs are determined by examining them in depth. The calculation of the Fuzzy Lean - Risk Priority Number (FL-RPN) is performed to rank the LFMs. A structured questionnaire has been developed to collect information from managers and industry experts for conducting FFMEA calculations. FL-RPN is calculated based on three key factors: occurrence (O), severity (S), and detection (D). Fuzzy numbers representing these factors are explained in Table 3.4, 3.5, and 3.6, along with the explanations for factors O, S, and D as well as linguistic variables (Ookalkar, 2009; Parameshwaran, 2018; Vijay Kumar & Chaturvedi, 2011). In the calculation of FFMEA, the relative weights of the risk factors are taken into account. The fuzzy numbers that represent this relative weight and the linguistic variables used to explain the risk factors are shown in Table 3.7 (Mandal & Maiti, 2014).
Fuzzy Numbers Related to the Occurrence of Lean Failure

Qualitative explanation for the occurrence	**Linguistic variables**	**Fuzzy numbers**
Even experienced people cannot recall remembering when it last happened.	Remote (R)	(1,1,1,2)
The individual with least experience tends to have a limited memory.	Low (L)	(1,2,3,4)
Many programed are recalled by experienced people, though only a handful stand out to them.	Moderate (M)	(3,4,6,7)
Repeated failures—all those involved remembers a lot.	High (H)	(6,7,8,9)
It almost all the time occurs; all individuals in the organization remembers a lot.	Very High (VH)	(8,9,10,10)

Table 4.4: Fuzzy Numbers Related to the Occurrence of Lean Failure

Qualitative description for severity	**Linguistic variables**	**Fuzzy numbers**
Inappropriate use or underuse of a resource that is not restrictive. A minimal increase in cost in the short term.	Moderately Very Low (MVL)	(1,1,2)
Delays in non-critical flows do not impact production—a slight cost increase in the short term.	Very Low (VL)	(1,2,3)

Duplicated information causes misunderstanding and wastes time determining the correct one.	Moderately Low (ML)	(2,3,4)
Delays in a least or a non-critical flow do not affect manufacturing. There will be an increase in cost in the medium term.	Low (L)	(3,4,5)
Duplicated and a repeated information leads to misunderstanding, loss of time, and additional cost to address the problem.	Moderately Medium (MM)	(4,5,6)
Delays in essential flows do affect the deadline of the service. A rise in expenses in the short-term.	Medium (M)	(5,6,7)
Inappropriate use or in sufficient utilization of a limited resources, Increase expenses in the medium-term.	Moderately Heigh (MH)	(6,7,8)
Delays in critical processes do affect the deadline of service. Increase in expenses in the medium-term.	Heigh (H)	(7,8,9)
Underutilizing or falling to fully utilize a limited resources leads to higher costs over time.	Moderately Very Heigh (MVH)	(8,9,10)
Delays in essential processes do impact service timelines. And a long-term cost will increase.	Very Heigh (VH)	(9,10,10)

Table 4.5: Fuzzy Numbers (Value) for the Occurrence of Lean Failure

Qualitative explanation for detection	**Linguistic Variables**	**Fuzzy numbers**
Identifying problems prior to a failure happening.	Moderately Very Low (MVL)	(1,1,2)
The chances of identifying problems before a failure happens is quite high.	Very Low (VL)	(1,2,3)
Likely to be identified before failure taking place	Moderately Low (ML)	(2,3,4)
There is a high likelihood of being detected prior failure occurs	Low (L)	(3,4,5)
The chances of detection before a failure happens are least.	Moderately Medium (MM)	(4,5,6)
Very little chance of being detected before the failure happens	Medium (M)	(5,6,7)

A comprehensive assessment after the detection of failure	Moderately Heigh (MH)	(6,7,8)
Assessment conducted around half of the time through the duration following the failure event.	Heigh (H)	(7,8,9)
Inspection for a little time, but it cannot prevent the occurrence of failure	Moderately Very Heigh (MVH)	(8,9,10)
Failure happens and there is no assessment	Very Heigh (VH)	(9,10,10)

Table 4.6: Fuzzy Numbers for Frequency of Lean Failure

Linguistic term	**Fuzzy Number**
Very Low (VL)	(0, 0.01, 0.24)
Low (L)	(0, 0.24, 0.5)
Medium (M)	(0.24, 0.5, 0.75)
Heigh (H)	(0.6, 0.75, 1)
Very Heigh (VH)	(0.74,1,1)

Table 4.7: Fuzzy Value for the Relative Weights of Risk Factors

The following paragraphs explain the FMEA calculations in detailed through a step-by-step procedure.

- Step 1: Compilation of linguistic perspectives from the FMEA team members

In this study, a fuzzy weighted geometric mean approach is used to **assess** the importance of each element in relation to one another. The aggregated subjective evaluation from experts can be computed by using equations (3.4) to (3.9). If the FMEA team consists of 'm' members TMJ ($j = 1, \ldots, m$) and is evaluating 'n' LFMs, LFMi ($i = 1, \ldots, n$), then:

$$\tilde{R}_i^o = \sum_{j=1}^{m} h_j \tilde{R}_{ij}^o = \left(\sum_{j=1}^{m} h_j \tilde{R}_{ijL}^o, \sum_{j=1}^{m} h_j \tilde{R}_{ijM_1}^o, \sum_{j=1}^{m} h_j \tilde{R}_{ijM_2}^o, \sum_{j=1}^{m} h_j \tilde{R}_{ijU}^o \right) i = 1, \ldots, n \quad (3.4)$$

$$\tilde{R}_i^s = \sum_{j=1}^{m} h_j \tilde{R}_{ij}^s = \left(\sum_{j=1}^{m} h_j \tilde{R}_{ijL}^s, \sum_{j=1}^{m} h_j \tilde{R}_{ijM}^s, \sum_{j=1}^{m} h_j \tilde{R}_{ijU}^s \right) \; i = 1, \ldots, n \quad (3.5)$$

$$\tilde{R}_i^D = \sum_{j=1}^{m} h_j \tilde{R}_{ij}^D = \left(\sum_{j=1}^{m} h_j \tilde{R}_{ijL}^D, \sum_{j=1}^{m} h_j \tilde{R}_{ijM}^D, \sum_{j=1}^{m} h_j \tilde{R}_{ijU}^D, \right) i = 1, \dots, n \ (3.6)$$

$$\widetilde{W}^O = \sum_{j=1}^{m} h_j \widetilde{W}_j^O = \left(\sum_{j=1}^{m} h_j \widetilde{W}_{jL}^O, \sum_{j=1}^{m} h_j \widetilde{W}_{jM}^O, \sum_{j=1}^{m} h_j \widetilde{W}_{jU}^O, \right) i = 1, \dots, n \ (3.7)$$

$$\widetilde{W}^S = \sum_{j=1}^{m} h_j \widetilde{W}_j^S = \left(\sum_{j=1}^{m} h_j \widetilde{W}_{jL}^S, \sum_{j=1}^{m} h_j \widetilde{W}_{jM}^S, \sum_{j=1}^{m} h_j \widetilde{W}_{jU}^S, \right) i = 1, \dots, n \ (3.8)$$

$$\widetilde{W}^D = \sum_{j=1}^{m} h_j \widetilde{W}_j^D = \left(\sum_{j=1}^{m} h_j \widetilde{W}_{jL}^D, \sum_{j=1}^{m} h_j \widetilde{W}_{jM}^D, \sum_{j=1}^{m} h_j \widetilde{W}_{jU}^D, \right) i = 1, \dots, n \ (3.9)$$

Where;

$\tilde{R}_{ij}^o = (\tilde{R}_{ijL}^o, \tilde{R}_{ijM_1}^o, \tilde{R}_{ijM_2}^o, \tilde{R}_{ijU}^o)$ is the fuzzy evaluation of FM_i on risk factor 'O' supplied by TM_j.

$\tilde{R}_{ij}^S = (\tilde{R}_{ijL}^S, \tilde{R}_{ijM}^S, \tilde{R}_{ijU}^o)$ is the fuzzy evaluation of FM_i on risk factor 'S' supplied by TM_j.

$\tilde{R}_{ij}^D = (\tilde{R}_{ijL}^D, \tilde{R}_{ijM}^D, \tilde{R}_{ijU}^D)$ is the fuzzy evaluation of FM_i on risk factor 'D' supplied by TM_j.

$\widetilde{W}_j^O = (\widetilde{W}_{jL}^O, \widetilde{W}_{jM}^O, \widetilde{W}_{jU}^O)$ is the fuzzy wait of risk factor 'O' supplied by TM_j

$\widetilde{W}_j^S = (\widetilde{W}_{jL}^S, \widetilde{W}_{jM}^S, \widetilde{W}_{jU}^S)$ is the fuzzy wait of risk factor 'S' supplied by TM_j

$\widetilde{W}_j^D = (\widetilde{W}_{jL}^D, \widetilde{W}_{jM}^D, \widetilde{W}_{jU}^D)$ is the fuzzy wait of risk factor 'D' supplied by TM_j

h_j (j = 1, …., m) is the significance of the weights assigned to FMEA team members must satisfying the condition $\sum_{j=1}^{m} h_j = 1$ with each $h_j > 0$ for j = 1, ……, m.

- Step 2: Elaborating on the Fuzzy Lean Risk Priority Number (FLRPN) for every LMF

FLRPN is calculated by taking relative weights of each risk factor through the subsequent equation. (Parameswaran et al., 2009).

$$FLRPN_i = \left(R_i^O\right)^{\frac{w^o}{w^o+w^s+w^D}} x \left(R_i^S\right)^{\frac{w^o}{w^o+w^s+w^D}} x \left(R_i^D\right)^{\frac{w^o}{w^o+w^s+w^D}} \ i = 1, \dots, n. \ (3.10)$$

Where, '*i*' represents the number of LFMs.

FLRPN$_i$ refers to the fuzzy lean risk priority number associated with failure mode 'i'.

R_i^O is the suggested fuzzy assessment or the rating of *LFMi* concerning the risk factor 'O'.
R_i^S is the suggested fuzzy assessment or the rating of *LFMi* concerning the risk factor 'S'.
R_i^D is the suggested fuzzy rating of *LFMi* concerning the risk factor 'D'.
W^O is the suggested fuzzy weight concerning the risk factor 'O' of *LFMi*.
W^S is the suggested fuzzy weight concerning the risk factor 'S' of *LFMi*.
W^D is the suggested fuzzy weight concerning the risk factor 'D' of *LFMi*.

- Step 3: Calculation of FLRPN using α level sets for each LFM

To prevent variability in experts' judgments caused by factors such as mood, environment, ambiance, or other influential factors, FLRPN is determined through α level sets. By adjusting different α values between 0 and 1, different $FLRPNi$ are generated. An α value of 0.5 is considered appropriate when the experts maintain a neutral mindset. The actions of an expert cannot be predicted; hence, the range of values from 0 to 1 is considered in this model. The equation below is used to determine the α level set values for the FLRPN of FMi (Wang et al., 2009):

$FLRPN_i = U_\alpha \, \alpha \, x \, [(FLRPN_i)_\alpha^L, (FLRPN_i)_\alpha^L], 0 < \alpha \leq 1$ (3.11)

Where,

$(FLRPN_i)_\alpha^L = \exp(Z_1^*)$ and $(FLRPN_i)_\alpha^U = \exp(Z_2^*)$

$Z_1^* \, and \, Z_2^*$ represents the optimal objective values determined through linear programming models as follow:

Min. $z_1 = \{u_1 \ln\left(R_i^0\right)_\alpha^L + u_2 \ln(R_i^S)_\alpha^L + u_3 \ln\left(R_i^D\right)_\alpha^L\}$ (3.12)

Subjected to $(u_1 + u_2 + u_3 = 1)$,
$(w^0)_\alpha^L * z \leq u_1 \leq (w^0)_\alpha^U * z,$
$(w^s)_\alpha^L * z \leq u_2 \leq (w^S)_\alpha^U * z,$
$(w^D)_\alpha^L * z \leq u_3 \leq (w^D)_\alpha^U * z,$
Here, $Z \leq 0$,

Max. $z_2 = \{u_1 \ln\left(R_i^0\right)_\alpha^L + u_2 \ln(R_i^S)_\alpha^L + u_3 \ln\left(R_i^D\right)_\alpha^L\}$ (3.13)

Subjected to $(u_1 + u_2 + u_3 = 1)$,
$(w^0)_\alpha^L * z \leq u_1 \leq (w^0)_\alpha^U * z,$
$(w^s)_\alpha^L * z \leq u_2 \leq (w^S)_\alpha^U * z,$
$(w^D)_\alpha^L * z \leq u_3 \leq (w^D)_\alpha^U * z,$
Here, $Z \leq 0$,
Where,

$\left[(R_i^0)_\alpha^L, (R_i^0)_\alpha^U\right]$ is the α-level set of combined 'O' rating,
$\left[(R_i^S)_\alpha^L, (R_i^S)_\alpha^U\right]$ is the α-level set of combined 'S' rating,
$\left[(R_i^D)_\alpha^L, (R_i^D)_\alpha^U\right]$ is the α-level set of combined 'D' rating,
$[(W^0)_\alpha^L, (W^0)_\alpha^U]$ is the α-level set of combined weight of 'O',
$[(W^S)_\alpha^L, (W^S)_\alpha^U]$ is the α-level set of combined weight of 'S',
$[(W^D)_\alpha^L, (W^D)_\alpha^U]$ is the α-level set of combined weight of 'D',

- Step 4: Defuzzied Centroid FLRPN

The fuzzy number corresponding the α-level set in FLRPN are represented in terms of intervals. Thus, the model employed the centroid defuzzification (CD) method. The CD of a fuzzy number in terms of the interval is computed using the following equation (Yager, 1981):

$$\bar{X}_0(\tilde{A}) = \frac{\int_a^d X\mu_{\tilde{A}}(X)dx}{\int_a^d \mu_{\tilde{A}}(X)dx} \quad (3.14)$$

Where,
$\bar{X}_0(\tilde{A})$ is the defuzzied value.
The defuzzified value can be expressed using its α-level sets as $\tilde{A}$ = U$_\alpha$ α.
$(A)_\alpha = U_\alpha\ \alpha \times [(X)_\alpha^L, (X)_\alpha^U]$ $(0 \leq \alpha \leq)$, the calculation of its defuzzified centroid can be performed using the condition $\Delta\alpha_i = 1/n$ and $\alpha_i = i/n$, i = 0, …..,n:

$$\int_a^d \mu_{\tilde{A}}(X)dx = \frac{1}{2n}\left[\left((X)_{\alpha_o}^U - (X)_{\alpha_o}^L\right) + \left((X)_{\alpha_n}^U - (X)_{\alpha_n}^L\right) + 2\sum_{i=1}^{n-1}\left((X)_{\alpha_i}^U - (X)_{\alpha_i}^L\right)\right] \quad (3.15)$$

$$\int_a^d X\mu_{\tilde{A}}(X)dx = \frac{1}{6n}\left[\left((X)_{\alpha_o}^{2U} - (X)_{\alpha_o}^{2L}\right) + \left((X)_{\alpha_n}^{2U} - (X)_{\alpha_n}^{2L}\right) + 2\sum_{i=1}^{n-1}\left((X)_{\alpha_i}^{2U} - (X)_{\alpha_i}^{L}\right)\right] + \frac{1}{6n}\sum_{i=0}^{n-1}\left((X)_{\alpha_i}^U * (X)_{\alpha_{i+1}}^U - (X)_{\alpha_i}^L * (X)_{\alpha_{i+1}}^L\right) \quad (3.16)$$

Equation (3.15) and (3.16) are applied to determine the centroid defuzzified values by equally dividing the interval [0, 1] using various α values. The calculated values are arranged in descending order. The highest value indicates the largest priority, and the lowest value has the lowest priority. The LFMs are ranked based on the centroid defuzzified values and will be presented to the management of the industry for discussion.

4.1.1.4..Stage 4: Lean Tools (LTs) identification and setting up an expert team focused on critical resources

The focused list of LFMs is reviewed with managers and experts within the organization, and the most important LFMs at the top of the list are considered for execution. Seeking consensus from the management and going deep into the literature review, the most suitable LTs are selected based on the cultural environment of the organization. After the literature review, management will be able to assign teams to concentrate on the specific critical resources, aiming to minimize waste. Only the prioritized LFMs are tackled in this first stage. Thus, it is expected that the prime causes will be eliminated at the time of executing lean practices. The focus is only on the critical LFMs, and no further calculations for the index are required (Souza & Carpinetti, 2014).

Shortcomings of Model 1 and opportunities for future modification

Though the model created meets the goals and objectives of the study, there are fields where it falls short in terms of completeness, as follows:

- Considering the lean management system's reliability, the model emphasized the importance of essential resources in stage 2. Only the top essential resources move forward to the next level, while the rest remain as they are.
- The risk associated with prioritizing critical resources (LFMs) is being explored in isolation; therefore, the risk diagnosis concerning other failure modes is not taken into account, which may have a significant impact on the industry's performance.
- In model 1, only recommendations taken on LTs are provided, along with a mutual understanding of managerial implications. However, the effectiveness of this model must be proved and confirmed with the future state.

4.2. Model 2: VSM Plant layout – Combined FFMEA Model

Model 1, explained in the previous section, combines FQFD and FFMEA with VSM and plant layout to scientifically prioritize LTs based on essential resources. However, in the end, some shortcomings were identified. Though the framed model met the objectives, some critiques remained unanswered. These identified shortcomings are addressed in model 2 by removing FQFD to prioritize critical resources. The second model takes into account the risks linked to every failure mode arising from critical resources.

Moving forward, with the support of experts from the organization, the growth and development of a future state map for assessing and validating the tool selection process is undertaken. In the following paragraphs, the development of model 2 is shown. The suggested model provides a three-stage procedure for selecting LTs, as explained in Figure 3.2.

- Stage 1: The current state VSM development and plant layout: Like the primary model, stage 1 centres on creating the current state VSM and plant layout. The details related to the production process are mapped into the current state VSM and plant layout, which engage with the real manufacturing environment. Since VSM and layout bring the wastes and sources of these wastes into view, they are used in the initial stage of this model. The current process is reviewed with the organization's decision-makers with the help of VSM and layout for its satisfactory level. If the organization is content with the current state, it will be continued, and this model ends there. If the performance is deemed unsatisfactory, stage 2 will be initiated, as explained in Figure 3.2.
- Stage 2: Wastes Identification, Critical Resources & Lfms, and And Ranking Them Using FFMEA: The VSM, plant layout, material, and information flow are used to identify the exact points of the wastes while concurrently examining the existing shop floor. The origins of the waste are also identified and considered critical resources. Further, the LFMs accountable for the generation of these wastes have been identified. Though the wastes are measured, it is not necessary that the outcomes are

always the same. The continuous waste generations are measured and recorded. The intermittent wastes are recorded with the assistance of expert experience and knowledge. This process is conducted by involving an FMEA study under a fuzzy context. Identification of the risk factors 'O', 'S,' and 'D' is made through questionnaires or by completing the FFMEA table.

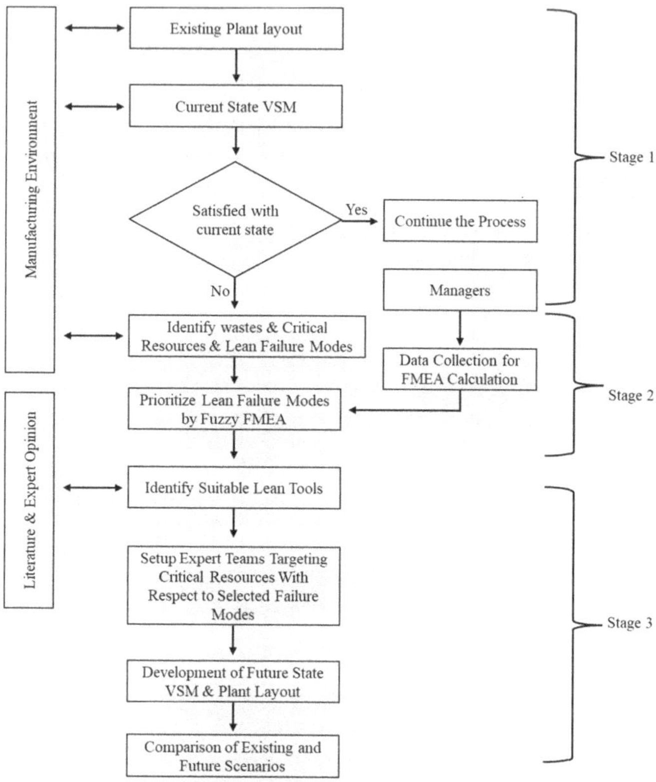

Figure 4.2: VSM Plant Layout – FFMEA Combined Model

4.2.1. Step 1: Gathering data for performing FFMEA evaluation

A check sheet is designed to gather all the data relevant to FFMEA computations. The collected information is used for evaluating and ranking LFMs in the FFMEA process. The risk factor values are determined by gathering experts' opinions using linguistic scales. The specialists, along with the organizational team members of FFMEA, have been assigned weights based on their ASK factors (Attitude, Skills, and Knowledge). These members also help in assigning the weight for each risk factor using linguistic terms. The linguistic terms associated with fuzzy ratings for risk factors, and weights given in model 1, are utilized.

4.2.2. Step 2: FFMEA evaluation

FFMEA calculations are performed following the specific procedures and equations given in stage 3 of model 1. The outcome of these calculations is the prioritized list of LFMs, which is then carried forward to the next stage.

4.2.3. Step 3: LTS Identification, Formation of Team of Experts, and Development of Future State VSM and Plant Layout

The identification of LTs is conducted through a literature review and by gathering various insights from organizational experts. The number of tools considered for execution is determined by threshold values set by the decision-makers of the organization. The tools linked with leading LFMs are considered, as executing all tools requires significant time and financial investment. The required resources linked to the selected LFMs are focused on employing experts from the organization. These experts receive guidelines to train and educate the staff on reducing waste.

To overcome the limitations identified in model 1, this model incorporates the development of the future state VSM and plant layout for model validation. The modifications are applied to the current state VSM and plant layout based on the forecast proposed by the organization. The computations for CT, UT, lead time, VA time, NVA time, the number of wastes, excess motions and transportations, and so on for future states are conducted with the help of decision-makers. After that, the current state is evaluated against the future state for its applicability.

4.2.3.1. Shortcomings of Model 2 and Opportunities for Improvement

Model 2 resolves the shortcomings found in model 1 by considering all the LFMs associated with the manufacturing process. Validation is made through redesigning and developing the future state and plant layout, but still, some criticisms are found in model 2:

- Critical resources are concentrated solely on the shortlisted LFMs. Hence, completeness cannot be guaranteed until all the resources are resolved.
- The selection of LTs is determined by the review of literature and recommendations from process owners. Each LT may influence others positively or negatively, and a single LT can address multiple FMs. Therefore, a scientific selection of LTs to tackle these concerns should be employed in the further development of the model.

4.3. Model 3: VSM Plant Layout – FFMEA – FAHP – FQFD Integrated General Model

Finally, the study presents a generic model integrating the current state VSM, plant layout, FFMEA, FAHP, FQFD, future state VSM, and plant layout. The model is structured into four stages, all explained in figure 3.3. The model is fine-tuned after two phases, addressing all the shortcomings identified in previous models. The model has been rectified to focus only on prioritizing LFMs and not on critical resources. Execution of LTs on LFMs alone would lead to positive improvements in resources. Therefore, the idea of focusing on the crucial resources is discarded; the extra efforts to modify all the required changes in all the critical resources are avoided.

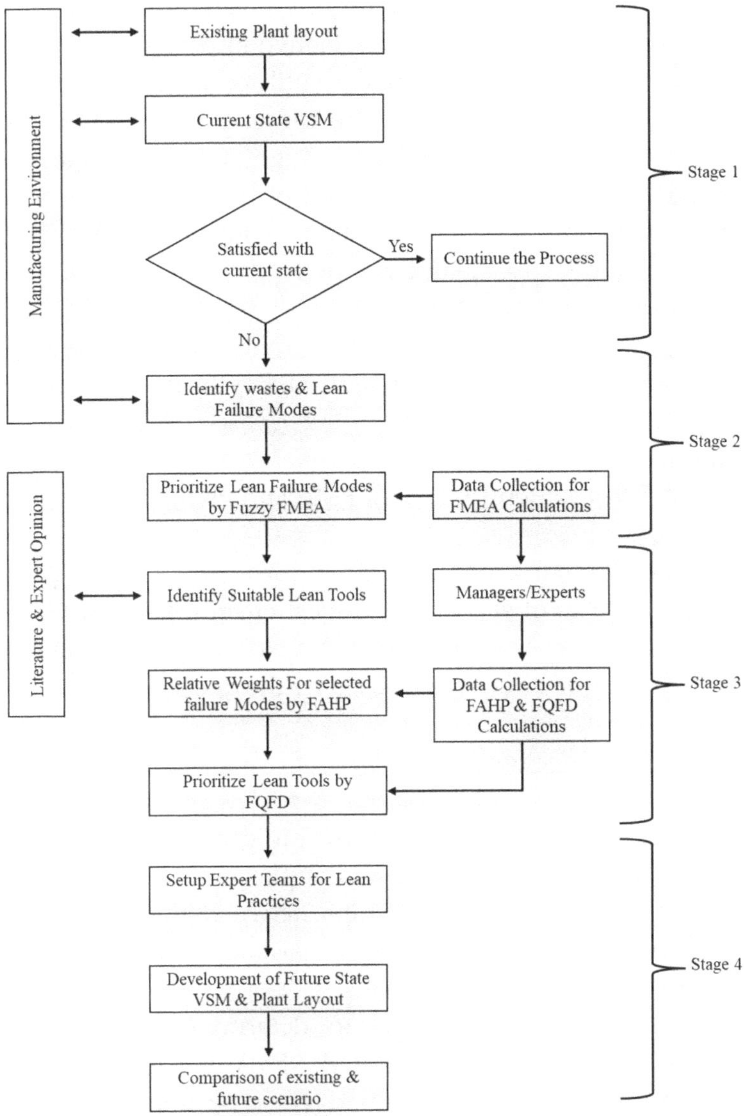

Figure 4.3: VSM Plant Layout – FFMEA – FAHP – FQFD Combined Model

FAHP and FQFD tools are integrated within the framework to facilitate the informed selection of LTs based on their appropriate situations for the production environment. In model 3, FFMEA is used to prioritise the LFMs by evaluating the associated risks. FAHP, a head-to-head comparison method, assigns relative importance and weights to the selected LFMs. These weights are utilised as the actual weights (Wi) of LFMs in FQFD calculations. The influence of one LT on another is also considered while ranking LTs through FQFD. The outcomes of FAHP and FQFD are the top-priority list of LTs. Just to compare the results, the future state VSM and the plant layout are created. The steps of this generic model are explained below.

4.3.1. Stage 1: Development of VSM (A Current State) and Plant Layout

Stage 1 is developing the current state VSM and the floor layout, which is the same as shown in model 2.

4.3.2. Stage 2: Wastes identification, LFMs, and giving priority to them using FFMEA

Stage 2 applies the equations and techniques shown in the previous model. The outcomes of stage 2 are the list of prioritised LFMs, and a selection of the top LFMs is made according to a threshold value set by the decision maker or directly proposed by the decision maker.

4.3.3. Stage 3: Identification and ranking of LTs using FAHP & FQFD

The identification of LTs is carried out by reviewing various literature and consulting with various experts, and to give priority to LTs, the focus is on their interrelationships and applicability to the real-world scenario, considering the relationships between the LTs and their associations with LFMs. This process consists of two phases: phase 1 and phase 2.

- Step 1: FAHP calculations to determine the comparative weights of LFMs. The selected LFMs are assigned relative weights using the FAHP method. These techniques evaluate the relative importance of one LFM compared to another. A pairwise comparison matrix is made to determine the relative weights. The linguistic terms and associated fuzzy numbers used for this evaluation are shown in table 3.8 (Somsuk & Laosirihongthong 2014).

For every industry expert, a pairwise comparison matrix ($\bar{A}$) constructed as

$$\tilde{A} = \begin{bmatrix} 1 & \tilde{a}_{12} & \dots & \tilde{a}_{1n} \\ \tilde{a}_{21} & 1 & \dots & \tilde{a}_{2n} \\ \dots & \dots & 1 & \dots \\ \tilde{a}_{n1} & \tilde{a}_{n2} & \dots & 1 \end{bmatrix} = \begin{bmatrix} (1,1,1) & (a_{12}, b_{12}, c_{12}) & \dots & (a_{1n}, b_{1n}, c_{1n}) \\ (a_{21}, b_{21}, c_{21}) & (1,1,1) & \dots & (a_{2n}, b_{2n}, c_{2n}) \\ \dots & \dots & \dots & \dots \\ (a_{n1}, b_{n1}, c_{n1}) & (a_{n2}, b_{n2}, c_{n2}) & \dots & (1,1,1) \end{bmatrix} \quad (3.17)$$

Where, $\tilde{a}_{ij}$ is represents an element of matrix ($\tilde{A}$) and it can take values in the matrix as $\tilde{a}_{ij} = (a_{ij}, b_{ij}, c_{ij}) = \frac{1}{c_{ij}}, \frac{1}{b_{ij}}, \frac{1}{a_{ij}}$ for i = 1,2,….n, j = 1,2,….n and i ≠ j and , $\tilde{a}_{ij}$ = (1,1,1) for i = j.

Weight (wi) Importance	**Fuzzy Number**
Equally (At par) Important (Eq)	(1;1;3)
Weakly (least) Important (Wk)	(1;3;5)
Essentially (fundamentally) Important (Es)	(3;5;7)
Very Strongly (bond) Important (Vs)	(5;7;9)
Absolutely (extremely) Important (Ab)	(7;9;9)

Table 8: Fuzzy Value for FAHP Computation

Similarly, a combined pairwise comparison matrix (PWCM) is created by combining all the distinguished matrices created by every expert. The resulting assumed pairwise comparison matrix ($\widetilde{M}$) contains the element ($\widetilde{M}_{ij}$), which is determined by

$\widetilde{M}_{ij} = (\tilde{a}_{ij}^{1} \times \tilde{a}_{ij}^{2} \times \dots \dots, \times \tilde{a}_{ij}^{E})^{1/E}$ (3.18)

Where E represents the number of experts from the different industry.

Next,

The fuzzy depiction of geometric mean matrix ($\tilde{r}_i$) is well defined from the matrix outcomes of equation (3.18) as

$\tilde{r}_i = (\widetilde{M}_{i1} \times \widetilde{M}_{i2} \times \dots \dots, \times \widetilde{M}_{in})^{1/n}$ (3.19)

Then the fuzzy relative weight of LFM'i' is represented as $\widetilde{W}_i = (L_{wi}, M_{wi}, U_{wi})$

Where, L_{wi} is the lower or the least value of $\widetilde{W}_i$ of ith LFM,

M_{wi} is the medium value of $\widetilde{W}_i$ of ith LFM,

U_{wi} is the upper or the highest value of $\widetilde{W}_i$ of ith LFM,

These computed values of relative weights (RW) are used directly in FQFD computations.

- Step 2: FQFD Calculations using FQFD to prioritize the most crucial LTs.

The selected LFMs are well placed in the "WHATs" section of the HoQ within the customer requirements panel, and the LTs are located in the "HOWs" section of the HoQ in the technical descriptors panel. The set-up objectives are to prioritize the most efficient LTs for reducing waste. The relative weights ($W\tilde{i}$) derived from the FAHP are used as Wi of LFMs in FQFD computations. The evaluation of a healthy relationship, correlation, and score calculations follows the same method as stage 2 in model 1. The priority list of LTs is reviewed with decision-makers, and LTs are suggested for execution based on their priority.

<u>4.4.4. Stage 4: VSM the Future State Mapping and the Plant Layout</u>

Below is the integration of the opted LFMs; the predicted future state is projected with the modifications. The calculated numbers derived from the predictions are recorded, and the changes are executed in the future state mapping. If required, the layout of the plant can also be changed based on recommendations made with the support of LTs.

4.4.4.1. Scope and limitations of VSM – Plant Layout -FFMEA – FAHP – FQFD combine general framework

The scope and constraints of this generic framework are mentioned below:

- Setting up a simultaneous analysis of VSM and the plant layout allows the decision-maker to anticipate the positive outcomes or drawbacks stemming from potential changes based on overall experience. This makes organizational members realize their ability to act and evaluate systematically in the current scenario.
- Adopting a fuzzy set for assessment helps in authentic evaluation of the ambiguous views of industry professionals. Typically, the professionals express their viewpoints about unwanted activities and involved risks through linguistic terms. Later, these verbal expressions are subsequently converted into fuzzy numbers for quantification. The prime

objective of adopting a fuzzy set is that the exact expressions are directly used for assessment.

- Considering the significance of risk factors like O, S, and D helps to differentiate the relevance of various LFMs.
- The explained model overcomes the various limitations of fuzzy mathematical calculations identified in the current literature. The use of a fuzzy weighted geometric mean approach makes this model more applicable in FFMEA assessment. Rather than using exact numbers, linguistic assessment provides relative importance weights for risk factors. In addition, the level of confidence of the assessors is taken into account through α-set levels, which improves the assessment and makes it more precise.
- Both the FAHP and the FQFD techniques are incorporated to facilitate a systematic selection of LTs that align with organizational needs, uplifting the model's structured techniques for LT selection.

4.5. Discussion and Conclusion

Implementing the lean concept in India's manufacturing and services industries primarily focuses on reducing waste and improving productivity, delivery, and quality to meet global standards at the least operating cost. Waste in manufacturing operations leads to excess working capital and hampers the organization's financial benefits. Identifying and ranking the critical factors as per their impact on lean implementation in the manufacturing sector is a multiple-criteria decision-making (MCDM) problem. The problem has been recognized, and a solution has been recommended using the hierarchical techniques described above. VSM, material flow layout, FQFD, and FFMEA together target the most crucial resources that generate significant production waste in the first model. The second model is introduced to address the limitations of the previous model. Later, in the third model, both the FAHP and the FQFD are fully employed to address the shortcomings of the second model. Thus, implementing the above models has made resource utilization effective.

Moreover, the successful implementation of lean in India's manufacturing and services industries has not only led to increased productivity, quality, delivery, and reduction in operating costs but has also demonstrated its potential for global impact. The financial benefits of using the VSM – Plant layout – FFMEA – FAHP – FQFD model, and the hypothesis formulated concerning the increment in productivity and its contribution to India's GDP, have been validated. The ranking obtained from AHP is a useful guide for industries worldwide, emphasizing critical fundamental issues while achieving the prescribed targets. This model paves the way for the ease of implementation of lean concepts in manufacturing and services organizations, not only in MSMEs but also in large industries around the globe, inspiring a global shift towards lean practices.

Chapter 5| Trends of MSME Sector Exports

5.1. Introduction

In previous chapters, we saw how lean manufacturing techniques are strategically crucial for Micro, Small, and Medium Enterprises. The Govt. has taken several programs to assist MSMEs in increasing their share of overall country exports. The Lean Manufacturing Competitiveness Scheme (LMCS) is one of them. Under LMCS, the government supports MSMEs pursuing lean manufacturing (LM) to uplift their efficiency and competitiveness by minimizing waste in manufacturing processes, inventory leveling, space optimization, energy efficiency and consumption, etc. Adopting lean manufacturing (LM) techniques results in cost savings for MSMEs. It also has many social benefits in terms of labor training, knowledge creation, labor productivity increments, lower input costs to other industries, the launch of new manufacturing equipment/methods in manufacturing, and the evaluation of work culture in society. LM techniques also result in reduced rejection, standardization of processes, and better layout of machines, leading to reduced excess motion and transportation of products during manufacturing, etc.

To achieve a sustained growth rate, the production and manufacturing sector must develop and maintain the competitiveness required to fulfill the challenges of globalization. Under the LM Scheme, SMEs have been assisted in manufacturing cost reductions by effectively managing people, optimizing space efficiently, inventory optimization and management, improved operational flows, reduced engineering time, etc., through the application of LM techniques. The execution of lean manufacturing techniques in enterprises has led to increasing returns to scale, i.e. (i) economies of scale that reduce per unit production cost, (ii) increased productivity of enterprises, and (iii) enhanced competitiveness in domestic and overseas markets. Simultaneously, it has also led to increased expertise in industries with respect to better work environments, managerial competencies, etc.

The MSME sector is an incredibly dynamic and thriving part of the Indian economy. With over 63 million units forming a vast network and providing employment for approximately 111 million people, it is a critical contributor to economic growth and development. The contribution of MSMEs to overall GDP for the fiscal years 2018-19 and 2019-20 was 30.5 percent and 30.0 percent, respectively, and for the financial year 2020-21, it dropped to 26.83 percent during the first year of the severe COVID pandemic (GOI, 2021). The sector accounted for annual merchandise exports of 45.04 percent in FY22 compared to 49.75 percent in FY20 and 49.35 percent in FY21, and around 40 percent of the country's total exports.

The current chapter will analyze MSME sector exports from India from 2005-06 to 2019-20. The performance of MSME sector exports vis-à-vis India's total exports is examined in section 5.2, and in the next section, the composition of MSME sector exports is discussed. The last part includes the chapter's final remarks.

5.2. MSME Export Performance

In the fiscal year 2005-06, exports from the MSME sector amounted to Rs. 6581 crores, rising to Rs. 24830 crores by 2019-20, which reflects a compound annual growth rate (CAGR) of nearly 10 percent throughout the study period. The comprehensive growth of the MSME sector in relation to India's total exports is shown in table 5.1 and figure 5.2.

As expressed in figure 4.1, exports from the MSME sector during the study period performed better than the overall exports. The aggregated exports from India grew from Rs. 19997 crores in 2005-06 to Rs. 49910 crores in 2019-20, which represented an increase of nearly 2.50 times. In contrast, the SME sector exports expanded from Rs. 6581 crores in 2005-06 to Rs. 24830 crores in 2019-20, reaching a growth rate of 3.77 times. The share of MSME sector exports in comparison to the aggregate exports was 32.91 percent in 2005-06, which grew to 49.47 percent by 2019-20. Throughout the study period, the MSME sector's average contribution to India's total export revenue was 34.34 percent.

Trends in India's MSME Exports – 2005-06 to 2019-20

Year	India's Total Exports (Rs. Crore)	% Increase in Total Exports	Exports of the MSME (Rs. Crore)	% Increase in exports from MSME	Share of MSME exports in total exports (%)
2004-05	16083	-	5330		33.14%
2005-06	19997	24.30%	6581	23.50%	32.91%
2006-07	25308	26.60%	8078	22.70%	31.92%
2007-08	28890	14.20%	8898	10.20%	30.80%
2008-09	27375	-5.20%	6978	-21.60%	25.49%
2009-10	37535	37.10%	10120	45.00%	26.96%
2010-11	44738	19.20%	14374	42.00%	32.13%
2011-12	44840	0.20%	19281	34.10%	43.00%
2012-13	47218	5.30%	15280	-20.80%	32.36%
2013-14	46835	-0.80%	15109	-1.10%	32.26%
2014-15	41679	-11.00%	13279	-12.10%	31.86%
2015-16	43964	5.50%	13893	4.60%	31.60%
2016-17	49826	13.30%	15845	14.00%	31.80%
2017-18	53864	8.10%	18411	16.20%	34.18%
2018-19	52924	-1.70%	25457	38.30%	48.10%
2019-20	49910	-5.70%	24830	-2.50%	49.75%
2020-21	66050	32.30%	32596	31.30%	49.35%

Table 5.1: Trends in India's MSME Exports – 2005-06 to 2019-20
Source –https://www.macrotrends.net/countries/IND/india/exports https://www.financialexpress.com/industry/sme/msme-eodb-msme-sectors-share-in-indias-gdp-drops- from-over-30-govt-data/2609856/

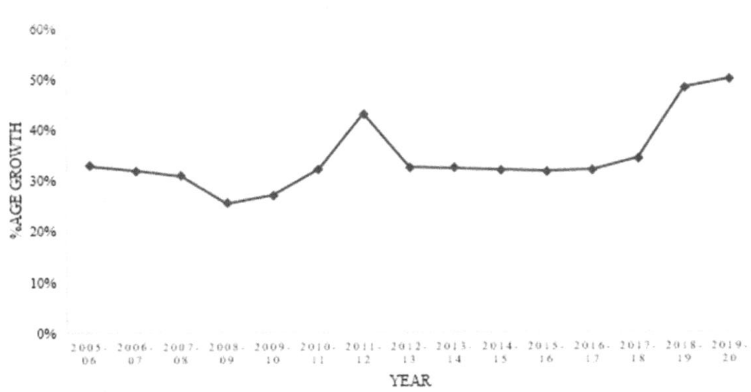

Figure 5.1: Annual Growth Rates Comparisons of Overall MSME Exports
Source – Calculated form Table 5.1

Figure 5.2: Share of MSME Exports in Total Exports of India
Source – Calculated form Table 5.1

However, investigating the year-on-year growth rate of exports from the MSME sector throughout the study period reveals that the growth was not consistent or uniform. Wide fluctuations characterized it. In 2009-10 and 2010-11, the MSME sector exports increased by 45.0 and 42 percent, respectively, the highest growth rates throughout the entire study period. As a result, India's aggregate exports also experienced their highest growth rate in the same year. The lowest growth rate documented for the MSME sector exports was in 2008-09, which was negative, due to the global crisis. The collapse of large investment banks worldwide, high oil prices, and rising inflation led to a global recession. India's trade deficit was dampened by negative import and export growth. India's total exports recorded the highest negative percentage in 2014-15, causing an economic slowdown. The aggregate exports from the MSME sector and overall exports revealed a positive trend from 2005-06 to 2019-20, although they experienced ups and downs. Throughout this research study timeframe, aggregate exports grew at an average annual growth rate of 8.62 percent. In comparison, exports from the MSME sector grew at an average annual growth rate of 12.85 percent during the same interval.

The rate of growth observed in India's aggregate exports during the study period was slightly lower than that of the exports from the MSME sector. This is further supported by comparing the CAGR of small- and medium-sized industries' exports with the country's total exports from the same study period. Over this period, the total exports experienced a compound growth rate of 6.75 percent yearly, while the MSME sector's exports expanded at a rate of 9.95 percent per year.

5.3. Composition of MSME Sector Exports

In the previous section, we had an overview of SME sector exports against the historical facts of India's overall exports. In this section, we investigate how the trends related to the output of the key export categories. Table 5.2 shows the trend of SME sector exports by two major categories, both traditional and non-traditional goods.

Figure 5.2 illustrates the timeframe from 2005-06 to 2019-20, when non-traditional products recorded an increase in their growth rate. Their value grew from Rs. 6243.59 crores in 2005-06 to Rs. 23586.67 crores in 2019-20, recording a growth of 3.78 times. In comparison, the rate of growth for traditional goods was recorded to be unfavourable for two years and exhibited greater fluctuation than that of non-traditional goods. It increased to Rs. 1243.23 crores in 2019-20 from Rs. 337.61 crores, representing a growth of 3.68 times. Additionally, the yearly average growth rate in exports from both traditional and non-traditional goods has been closely identical across the study period.

Trends in Major Categories of MSME Export from India

Year	Total MSME Exports		Non-Traditional Goods		Traditional Goods	
	Value (Rs. Crore)	% Rate of Growth	Value (Rs. Crore)	% Rate of Growth	Value (Rs. Crore)	% Rate of Growth
2005-06	6581	-	6243.59	-	337.61	-
2006-07	8078	22.75%	7728.47	23.78%	349.53	3.53%
2007-08	8898	10.15%	8531.67	10.39%	366.33	4.81%
2008-09	6978	-21.58%	6655.34	-21.99%	322.66	-11.92%
2009-10	10120	45.03%	9640.32	44.85%	479.68	48.66%
2010-11	14374	42.04%	13820.96	43.37%	553.04	15.30%
2011-12	19281	34.14%	18547.11	34.20%	733.89	32.70%
2012-13	15280	-20.75%	14718.89	-20.64%	561.11	-23.54%
2013-14	15109	-1.12%	14156.20	-3.82%	952.80	69.81%
2014-15	13279	-12.11%	12261.69	-13.38%	1017.31	6.77%

2015-16	13893	4.62%	13197.33	7.63%	695.62	-31.62%
2016-17	15845	14.05%	15319.31	16.08%	525.69	-24.43%
2017-18	18411	16.19%	17847.84	16.51%	562.95	7.09%
2018-19	25457	38.27%	23506.73	31.71%	1950.27	246.44%
2019-20	24830	-2.46%	23586.67	0.34%	1243.23	-36.25%

Table 5.2: Trends in Major Categories of MSME Export from India
Source: Manual of industrial Policy and Statistics, Office of the Economic Advisor Ministry of Commerce, and Industry Government of India, New Delhi

The nontraditional goods exports experienced a yearly average growth rate of 12.07 percent, whereas the traditional goods revealed a high growth rate of 21.95 percent yearly from 2015-16 to 2019-20.

However, the disparity becomes significant when we investigate the compounded annual growth rate of exports from both the traditional and nontraditional goods. During the period 2005-06 to 2019-20, the compounded annual growth rate of nontraditional goods exports originating from the MSME sector was estimated at 09.96 percent, while traditional goods exports showed an annual growth rate of 09.76 percent.

Therefore, the nontraditional exports played a more important role in the overall goods exports of the MSME sector than the traditional goods exports. The entire scenario has proven to be essential for export promotion. The reality is also established from their contributions to the total MSME sector exports.

Going through Table 5.3 below, it shows that the proportion of the nontraditional goods categories within the total MSME sector exports rose from 94.87 percent in 2005-06 to 94.99 percent in 2019-20. In contrast, the share of traditional goods slightly decreased to 05.01 percent in 2019-20 from 05.13 percent in 2005-06.

Proportion of Traditional and Non – Traditional Commodity

Year	Non-Traditional (%)	Traditional (%)	Total (%)
2005-06	94.87	5.13	100.00
2006-07	95.67	4.33	100.00
2007-08	95.88	4.12	100.00
2008-09	95.38	4.61	100.00
2009-10	95.26	4.73	100.00
2010-11	96.15	3.84	100.00

2011-12	96.18	3.82	100.00
2012-13	96.34	3.66	100.00
2013-14	93.68	6.32	100.00
2014-15	92.33	7.67	100.00
2015-16	94.98	5.02	100.00
2016-17	96.67	3.33	100.00
2017-18	96.93	3.07	100.00
2018-19	92.34	7.66	100.00
2019-20	94.99	5.01	100.00

Table 5.3: Proportion of Traditional and Non – Traditional Commodity Group in Overall MSME Exports: 2005-06 to 2019-20

Source: Calculated form Table 5.2

Thus, the analysis shown above demonstrates that the initiatives of the goods exports of the MSME sector in India align with the required priorities of the group of nontraditional commodity exports, which is also our country's top priority.

The timeframe used for comparison is 2005-06 to the year 2019-20. The goods selected for this analysis from both the traditional and nontraditional categories are listed as follows:

- **Traditional or classic goods:**
  - ✓ Cashew nuts and the extracted liquid from the cashew
  - ✓ Lac, and
  - ✓ Spices, oils from spices, oleoresins
- **Non–Traditional or conventional goods:**
  - ✓ Engineering goods
  - ✓ Basic chemicals, pharmaceuticals, and cosmetics
  - ✓ Products related to chemicals and allied products
  - ✓ Plastic products
  - ✓ Finished leather and leather products
  - ✓ Marine products
  - ✓ Processed foods
  - ✓ Woollen clothing and knitwear
  - ✓ Sports goods
  - ✓ Readymade garments
  - ✓ Products made from rayon and synthetic materials
  - ✓ Processed tobacco, snuff, and bidi, and

✓ Electronic or digital and computer application software

As can be seen from the analysis presented in Table 5.4, it has been observed that, during the study period, the export revenue from nontraditional goods outpaced that of traditional goods in terms of growth. Particularly, the export earnings for nontraditional goods increased to Rs. 493434.93 crores in 2019-20, up from Rs. 118293.50 crores in 2005-06, recording a compounded growth rate of 9.980 percent yearly. At the same time, traditional goods recorded a higher compounded growth rate (CGR) of 11.591 percent yearly, growing from Rs. 2166.332 crores in 2005-06 to Rs. 11230.881 crores in 2019-20 in absolute value.

However, within these two expanded categories, the performance of exports differed significantly from one good to another.

A. Non - Traditional (Rs. Crore)									
Sr. No.	Product Group	Total Exports		Exports form MSME		% Share of Exports from MSME		CAGR % for Total Exports	CAGR % for MSME Exports
		2005-06	2019-20	2005-06	2019-20	2005-06	2019-20	2005-2020	2019-2020
1	Engineering Goods	40759.51	240721.24	12322.64	78991.30	30.23	32.81	12.57	13.19
2	Basic Chemicals, Pharmaceutical & Cosmetics	23220.07	139075.61	12771.29	61901.82	55.00	44.51	12.67	11.10
3	Chemical & Allied Products	10728.89	25435.90	301.87	8510.76	2.81	33.46	5.92	24.93
4	Plastic Products	4782.90	54875.68	2153.29	22871.00	45.02	41.68	17.66	17.06
5	Finished Leather & Leather Products	9394.60	22339.02	7515.88	24650.00	80.00	110.35	5.94	8.24
6	Marine Products	7362.67	28665.01	2111.24	13543.08	28.67	47.25	9.48	13.19
7	Processed Foods	14795.96	158235.53	9616.80	110769.45	65.00	70.00	17.11	17.70
8	Woolen Garments & Knitwear	1379.23	2989.45	482.63	2841.02	34.99	95.03	5.29	12.54
9	Sports Goods	339.19	1148.75	339.19	1148.75	100.00	100.00	8.47	8.47
10	Ready-made Garments	27825.35	81847.60	25042.75	73661.26	90.00	90.00	7.46	7.46
11	Rayon & Synthetic Products	8357.77	17718.47	5516.13	16650.00	66.00	93.97	5.14	7.64
12	Processed Tobacco & Snuff and Bidi	1140.62	2394.92	539.42	1516.48	47.29	63.32	5.07	7.13
13	Electronic & Computer Software	55747.00	254206.32	39580.37	76380.00	71.00	30.05	10.64	4.48
14	**Total of A**	**205833.76**	**1029653.48**	**118293.50**	**493434.93**	**57.47**	**47.92**	**11.32**	**9.98**

B. Traditional Products (Rs. Crore)									
Sr. No.	Product Group	Total Exports		Exports form MSME		% Share of Exports from MSME		CAGR % for Total Exports	CAGR % for MSME Exports
		2005-06	2019-20	2005-06	2019-20	2005-06	2019-20	2005-2020	2019-2020
1	Cashew Kernel & Cashew Nutshell Liquid	2176.20	6963.84	1866.27	7963.84	85.75	114.35	8.06	10.15
2	Lac	109.08	305.42	106.80	330.42	97.9	108.18	7.1	7.82
3	Spices, Spices oils, Oleoresins	1933.20	9859.32	193.27	2936.62	9.99	29.78	11.47	19.88
Total of B		**4218.48**	**17128.58**	**2166.337**	**11230.884**	**51.35**	**65.56**	**9.79**	**11.59**
Grand Total of (A+B)		**210052.24**	**1046782.07**	**120459.84**	**504665.81**	**51.65**	**48.80**	**11.24**	**11.50**

Table 5.4: CAGR and the Proportion of Selected Goods in India's Overall Exports

Source – (1.) SIDBI Report on Micro Small and Medium Enterprises, SIDBI, 2021, Lucknow;
(2.) National Small industries Corporation; www.nsic.co.in (3.) Office of the Development Commissioner, MSME, Govt. of India, New Delhi

A. Non - Traditional (In Percent)

Sr. No.	Product Group	Years														
		2005-06	2006-07	2007-08	2008-09	2009-10	2010-11	2011-12	2012-13	2013-14	2014-15	2015-16	2016-17	2017-18	2018-19	2019-20
1	Engineering Goods	9.99	10.93	11.65	14.53	15.01	15.52	15.23	15.12	15.22	15.53	15.69	15.71	15.88	16.01	16.01
2	Basic Chemicals, Pharmaceutical & Cosmetics	11.34	11.03	11.28	11.23	11.20	11.19	11.20	11.18	11.17	11.16	11.15	10.17	11.14	11.11	11.17
3	Chemical & Allied Products	0.95	0.76	0.6	3.9	3.73	3.92	4.51	4.58	4.20	4.31	4.52	4.52	4.72	4.69	4.69
4	Plastic Products	1.81	2.44	2.64	2.17	2.59	2.71	2.84	2.97	3.10	3.23	3.35	3.37	3.31	3.33	3.27
5	Finished Leather & Leather Products	6.63	6.71	8.02	7.1	7.80	8.07	7.81	8.61	8.88	8.15	8.21	8.21	8.02	8.07	8.07
6	Marine Products	4.17	3.87	3.67	3.78	3.53	3.39	3.26	3.12	2.98	2.85	2.71	2.71	2.66	2.58	2.47
7	Processed Foods	8.1	8.9	9.68	11.25	10.81	11.42	11.52	11.62	11.13	11.55	11.63	11.63	11.59	11.61	11.59
8	Woolen Garments & Knitwear	3.7	3.86	3.29	1.42	1.22	1.31	1.30	1.50	1.61	1.33	1.39	1.39	1.32	1.32	1.32
9	Sports Goods	0.43	0.36	0.39	0.37	0.35	0.34	0.32	0.31	0.29	0.28	0.26	0.27	0.27	0.27	0.29
10	Ready-made Garments	39.82	38.15	34.94	27.21	24.77	22.67	21.56	21.46	21.40	21.31	21.45	21.47	21.49	21.57	21.52
11	Rayon & Synthetic Products	1.63	1.81	1.83	1.73	1.83	1.86	1.89	1.93	1.96	1.99	1.45	1.45	1.47	1.47	1.43
12	Processed Tobacco & Snuff and Bidi	1.36	0.91	0.79	0.78	0.50	0.62	0.79	0.88	0.72	0.55	0.62	0.62	0.71	0.77	0.82
13	Electronic & Computer Software	2.39	5.26	7.89	10.46	12.73	13.19	12.83	13.69	13.87	13.01	13.52	13.63	13.72	14.02	13.08
14	**Total of A**	**92.32**	**94.99**	**96.67**	**95.93**	**96.045**	**96.208**	**95.061**	**96.954**	**96.531**	**95.235**	**95.953**	**95.148**	**96.3**	**96.82**	**95.73**

B. Traditional Products (In Percent)

Sr. No.	Product Group	Years														
		2005-06	2006-07	2007-08	2008-09	2009-10	2010-11	2011-12	2012-13	2013-14	2014-15	2015-16	2016-17	2017-18	2018-19	2019-20
1	Cashew Kernel & Cashew Nutshell Liquid	4.54	2.69	2.29	2.52	2.02	2.69	2.29	2.32	2.52	2.52	2.69	2.29	2.32	2.39	2.52
2	Lac	0.15	0.19	0.2	0.66	1.12	0.19	1.72	0.66	0.51	1.12	0.19	1.72	0.66	0.51	1.12
3	Spices, Spices oils, Oleoresins	2.99	2.13	0.84	0.89	0.82	1.13	0.84	0.41	0.89	0.82	1.13	0.84	0.41	0.62	0.82
Total of B		**7.68**	**5.01**	**3.33**	**4.07**	**3.96**	**4.01**	**4.85**	**3.39**	**3.92**	**4.46**	**4.01**	**4.85**	**3.39**	**3.52**	**4.46**
Grand Total of (A+B)		**100**	**100**	**100**	**100**	**100**	**100**	**100**	**100**	**100**	**100**	**100**	**100**	**100**	**100**	**100**

Table 5.5: Percentage Share of Principal Items of Micro Small and

Medium Enterprises Exports of India
Source – (1.) SIDBI Report on Micro Small and Medium Enterprises, SIDBI, 2021, Lucknow; (2.)

National Small industries Corporation; www.nsic.co.in (3.) Office of the Development Commissioner, MSME, Govt. of India, New DelhiAmong traditional goods, the export trend for cashew kernels, liquid cashew nutshell, spices, oil from spices, and oleoresins remained stable except for the last three years. In the study timeframe, the absolute figures for lac presented a variable trend. At the same time, exports in nontraditional categories like engineering goods, basic lubricants and chemicals, pharmaceuticals, chemical and related products, sports goods, electronics, and software have shown relatively consistent and stable trends. The rest of the nontraditional goods exports experienced variable trends.

Table 5.5 shows the percent contribution of selected traditional and nontraditional goods within the gross from the MSME sector. The share of traditional goods fell by nearly 3 percent, dropping from 7.68 percent in 2005-06 to 4.46 percent in 2019-20, while the share of nontraditional products rose by just over 3 percent across the study period.

The proportion of specific products within overall MSME exports showed significant variation across the study period. In the traditional product category, the shares of cashew kernels, liquid cashew nutshell, and spices experienced significant fluctuations, and their shares declined in 2019-20 compared to the base year 2005-06. However, the contribution of lac increased from 0.15 percent in 2005-06 to 1.12 percent in 2019-20. In the category of nontraditional items, the share of electronic goods rose from 9.990 percent in 2005-06 to 16.01 percent in 2019-20. The shares of chemical and related products, plastic products, finished leather and leather goods, processed food, and electronic and computer application software grew by 0.95, 1.81, 6.63, 8.1, and 2.39 percent, respectively, in 2005-06 to 16.01, 4.69, 3.27, 8.07, 11.59, and 13.08 in 2019-20. The proportion of chemicals, medicines, and beauty products declined from 11.34 percent in 2005-06 to 11.17 percent in 2019-20. The shares of marine products, woollen garments, sports goods, ready-made garments, rayon & synthetic products, and chemically processed tobacco significantly declined. However, their contributions fluctuated greatly during the study timeframe.

The growing significance of specific selected product exports from the MSME sector is underscored by their contribution to the overall exports of these goods from India. Table 5.4 shows the country's total exports of key commodities from 2005-06 to 2019-20. It also indicates the share of the MSME sector in India's exports of these primary items over the same timeframe.

The MSME export performance of the respective sector vis-à-vis the total exports of the specific commodities is analysed using the data provided in Table 5.4.

- **Engineering Goods:** The SME sector exported various engineering goods valued at Rs. 12322.640 crores in 2005-06, which grew to Rs. 78991.310 crores by 2019-20, reflecting a compound annual growth rate of 13.19 percent. In comparison, the total exports of this category experienced a lower compound annual growth rate of 12.57 percent. The share of engineering goods exports from the MSME sector saw a slight increase from 30.230 percent in 2005-06 to 32.810 percent in 2019-20.
- **Basic Chemicals, Medicines, and Cosmetics:** In the financial year 2005-06, exports of the MSME sector in this category amounted to Rs. 12771.29 crores, which increased to Rs. 61901.820 crores in 2019-20. It presented a compound annual growth rate of 11.10 percent, which was lower than the total export growth of this category during 2005-06 to 2019-20. Its proportion of total exports declined from 55 percent to 44.51 percent during the same timeframe.
- **Chemical and Related Products:** Exports of chemical and related products from the MSME sector were Rs. 301.870 crores in 2005-06 and rose to Rs. 8510.760 crores in 2019-20. This sector recorded a compound annual growth rate of 24.930 percent, significantly exceeding the gross export compounded growth rate (CGR) of 5.920 percent annually. Moreover, its contribution to gross exports grew from 2.810 percent in 2005-06 to 33.460 percent in 2019-20. However, the export figures for this vertical in 2019-20 were considerably higher than in previous years, which contributed to the excellent growth rate and share in overall exports.

- **Plastic Products:** The exports of plastic products from the MSME segment were Rs. 2153.29 crores in 2005-06 and increased to Rs. 22871 crores in 2019-20, reflecting a CAGR of 17.06 percent over this timeframe. The registered growth rate fell short of the total export growth for this category. Furthermore, its contribution to total exports decreased to 41.670 percent in 2019-20 from 45.020 percent in 2005-06.
- **Finished Leather and Related Products:** Exports in this category varied throughout the study timeframe. In 2005-06, exports amounted to Rs. 7515.88 crores, which further grew to Rs. 24650.00 crores in 2019-20, recording a CAGR of 8.24 percent. However, the overall CAGR of this item was lower at 5.940 percent annually. The proportion of goods exports from this sector compared to total exports of these categories rose significantly from 80.00 percent in 2005-06 to 110.350 percent in 2019-20.
- **Marine Products:** Exports of marine goods increased steadily, reaching Rs. 13543.08 crores in 2019-20, up from Rs. 2111.24 crores in 2005-06. It recorded a higher CAGR than the overall exports in this vertical, at 13.19 percent throughout the study period. The contribution of MSME sector exports within the overall exports of marine products rose from 28.67 percent in 2005-06 to 47.25 percent in 2019-20.
- **Processed Food:** In 2005-06, the export value of processed food from the respective sectors was Rs. 9616.80 crores, which increased to Rs. 110769.45 crores by 2019-20. This significant growth occurred at a CAGR of 17.70 percent, which was higher than the total export growth of this item. In 2019-20, the total export of processed food amounted to Rs. 158235.53 crores, with the SME sector contributing approximately 70 percent of this total. This sector's contribution was nearly 65.00 percent in 2005-06.
- **Woollen Garments and Woollen Clothing:** Exports of this item were Rs. 482.63 crores in 2005-06, which grew significantly to Rs. 2841.02 crores in 2019-20, reflecting a CAGR of 12.54 percent. However, the overall export of this product experienced modest growth of only 5.29 percent annually from 2005-06 to 2019-20.

The MSME sector contribution to the overall exports of this product increased significantly from 34.99 percent in 2005-06 to 95.03 percent in 2019-20.

- ✓ **Sports Goods:** The exports of sports goods from the SME sector amounted to Rs. 339.19 crores in the year 2005-06 and increased to Rs. 1148.75 crores by the year 2019-20, registering a CAGR of 8.47 percent. During the study timeframe, the MSME sector contributed nearly 100 percent to the total exports of sports products.
- ✓ **Ready-made Garments:** The exports of ready-made garments increased from Rs. 25042.75 crores in 2005-06 to Rs. 73661.26 crores in 2019-20. The overall rate of export growth for total exports and the MSME sector was 7.46 percent during the study period. While the share percentage of MSME sector exports in the total ready-made garment exports remained the same in both the financial years 2005-06 and 2019-20, it also experienced fluctuations throughout the timeframe.
- ✓ **Rayon and Synthetic Products:** In the financial year 2005-06, the exports of rayon and synthetic products were Rs. 5516.13 crores, which saw a considerable increase to Rs. 16650.0 crores by 2019-20, registering a CAGR of 7.64 percent yearly during the same timeframe. The contribution of the MSME sector in overall exports went up from 66.00 percent in the year 2005-06 to 93.97 percent in the year 2019-20.
- ✓ **Tobacco Products, Snuff, and Bidi:** From the financial year 2005-06 to 2019-20, exports from this sector within these categories increased from Rs. 539.42 crores to Rs. 1516.48 crores. This growth registered a CAGR of 7.13 percent compared to the overall export growth of only 5.07 percent during the study period. The contribution of the MSME sector in the overall exports of this product grew significantly from 47.29 percent in 2005-06 to 63.33 percent in 2019-20.
- ✓ **Electronic and Computer Application Software:** The value of exports of this item was Rs. 39580.37 crores in 2005-06 and recorded a significant increase to Rs. 76380.00 crores in 2019-20, registering a CAGR of 4.48 percent over the years from 2005-06

to 2019-20. The contribution of the MSME sector in the total exports of this category dropped from 71.00 percent in 2005-06 to 30.05 percent in 2019-20.

Total non-traditional exports amounted to Rs. 118293.50 crores in 2005-06, which went up to Rs. 493434.93 crores in 2019-20. It registered a CAGR of 9.98 percent during the same timeframe. However, the MSME sector's contribution to the total exports of these items from India slightly dropped from 57.47 percent in 2005-06 to 47.92 percent in 2019-20.

- ✓ **Cashew Kernel and Cashew Nutshell Liquid:** Exports of this product were Rs. 1866.27 crores in the year 2005-06, which further increased to Rs. 7963.84 crores in the financial year 2019-20, registering a CAGR of 10.15 percent yearly during the same timeframe. The contribution of MSME sector exports in total exports of this product was approximately 114.35 percent during the overall period, except in the year 2005-06, where it was 85.75 percent.
- ✓ **Lac:** In the financial year 2005-06, lac exports were Rs. 106.80 crores, which steadily grew to Rs. 330.42 crores in 2019-20. It recorded a CAGR of 7.82 percent. The contribution of the MSME sector in total exports of lac was nearly 108.18 percent during the same period.
- ✓ **Spices, Spice Oils, Oleoresins:** The exports of this product category increased from Rs. 193.27 crores in the financial year 2005-06 to Rs. 2936.62 crores in the year 2019-20, registering a CAGR of 19.88 percent yearly. At the same time, overall exports from this category registered a CAGR of 11.47 percent during the years 2005-06 to 2019-20. The contribution of the MSME sector in overall exports of these items was 9.99 percent in 2005-06 and 29.78 percent in 2019-20.

In the financial year 2005-06, the total exports of traditional goods from the MSME sector were Rs. 2166.33 crores, which further went up to Rs. 11230.88 crores by 2019-20. During the study period, it recorded a CAGR of 11.59 percent. The MSME sector contribution to the overall exports of traditional goods increased from 51.35 percent in 2005-06 to 65.56 percent in 2019-20.

5.3. Conclusion

Lean manufacturing is the best management technique for improving MSMEs' performance in the 21st-century global competitive market. Research studies have shown that it produces higher quality, productivity, and customer responsiveness. The organization must concentrate on the whole value chain by implementing comprehensive tools to secure the full benefits of lean manufacturing.

While large organizations may find it easier to adopt lean principles, MSMEs, with their resource constraints, can also implement lean manufacturing. The key lies in leveraging employee involvement to introduce feasible practices and low-cost tools such as workplace management, visual management, visual control, and Kanban without a computerized system.

For MSMEs, it is crucial to take immediate steps to strengthen their internal capabilities. One effective strategy is to appoint a lean management representative who can oversee the entire lean process and conduct in-house training on specific principles and practices.

As an alternative, MSMEs should actively collaborate with the primary customer on lean practices. Innovative partnerships between raw material or product suppliers and the customer in lean manufacturing could benefit both partners.

Since limited research has been conducted on the fundamental lean practices in MSMEs, I have studied the impact of the fundamental lean practices that are feasible to implement in MSMEs and the impact of the proposed lean model on the growth of MSME exports and its contribution to India's GDP.

Based on the above study, the CAGR recorded by India's overall exports was lower than the rate of growth achieved by the MSME sector exports during the period of study. Between the two main categories of exports from the MSME sector, non-traditional goods exports showed high fluctuations and contributed slightly less to overall MSME sector exports compared to traditional goods. Moreover, within the MSME sector, five items alone represented nearly 81.41 percent of total exports in 2019-20. These products were readymade garments (14.93 percent), engineering goods (16.01 percent), electronic and computer application software (15.48 percent), processed foods (22.45 percent), and basic chemicals, pharmaceuticals, and cosmetics (12.55 percent).

The MSME sector has made a significant contribution to total exports across various product categories: sports goods (100 percent), woollen garments and related products (95.03 percent), readymade garments (90 percent), processed foods (70 percent), finished leather and leather products (110.35 percent), processed tobacco, snuff, and bidi (63.32 percent), marine products (47.25 percent), basic chemicals, pharmaceuticals, and cosmetics (44.51 percent), and plastic products (41.68 percent).

In the traditional product vertical, products such as cashew kernel, liquid cashew nutshell, and lac contributed 104.35 and 108.18 percent, respectively, to India's exports.

The MSME sector has shown remarkable adaptability and potential in the non-traditional vertical, with a CAGR of 9.98 percent for exports, slightly below the 11.32 percent for overall exports.

The MSME sector has also demonstrated its resilience and competitiveness in the traditional product vertical, with a CAGR of 11.59 percent for exports, outperforming the 9.79 percent for overall exports.

Exports from the MSME sector recorded a CAGR of 11.50 percent against the overall export growth of 11.24 percent during the post-study period.

Therefore, the above analysis of facts and figures reveals that implementing lean techniques in exporting MSMEs plays a significant role in the Indian economy. With the government's initiatives on the lean manufacturing competitiveness program and public sector support, MSMEs have the potential to take India to new heights. By providing the right quality of products in the correct quantity at the right time and satisfying the end customers, MSMEs are expected one day to overtake strong competitor nations in terms of volume. Furthermore, the export performance and competitiveness of Indian MSMEs can be improved by working on the critical performance areas of the sector and overcoming key challenges, as the new economic reforms and policies have accelerated the degree of competitiveness. Hence, there is an urgent need to convert threats into opportunities.

Chapter 6| Problem and Prospects of Lean Implementations and MSME Sector Exports

6.1. Introduction

The preceding chapter's analysis of lean implementation and its impact on India's exports from the micro, small, and medium-sized enterprise sectors indicates that the increase in exports did not follow an incremental trend. The CAGR of exports from the micro, small, and medium-sized enterprise sectors has been significantly higher compared to the total exports from India during the study period from 2005-06 to 2019-20. However, when investigating the main export items from the MSME sector in comparison to the total exports of these products, a contradictory situation emerges. The contribution of MSMEs among the industrial segments that export these products has reduced, and the CAGR has remained relatively low in comparison to the total exports during the study period.

This chapter aims to identify the challenges faced during lean implementation and the factors that affect exports from the micro, small, and medium enterprises sector that hinder their potential and the setting up of a consistent trend. This research study is essential as it will also enable us to evaluate the various possibilities and recommendations over strategies to enhance export prospects, thereby highlighting the necessity for additional research in this area.

6.2. Problems with Exports

Exports from micro, small, and medium-sized enterprises face two categories of problems:

6.2.1. External Problems

Because of the liberalization of India's economy initiated by the economic reforms of 1991 and India's entry into the WTO, it is expected that the micro, small, and medium-sized enterprise sectors will encounter challenges that may adversely affect Indian export trade unless they enhance their competitiveness. Even after three decades of economic reforms, the impact of globalization on MSME exports, as experienced/anticipated, is as follows:

- Because of the liberalization of global markets through free trade, which has involved reducing tariffs and dismantling various other restrictions in all participating countries, competition in global trade has increased, and it is becoming tough to procure export orders to the benefit of the micro, small, and medium-sized industry sector.
- Only the traders who are engaged in export and import gain an advantage and benefit from a clearer regulatory environment, enabling them to offer customers top-quality products at more reasonable and competitive prices.
- When quantitative restrictions on imports were eliminated by the end of March 2001 as per India's commitment to the WTO, the Exim Policy of the Govt. of India proved to be ineffective. This seriously impacted exports from the MSME sector during the initial stage of the study period, as the advantage provided by various schemes available to them vanished.
- The agreement related to subsidies and countervailing measures restricts the majority of export subsidies, allowing only those products that are aggregable, which were intended to be phased out by 2014 under the global trade policy for 2009-14. In this scheme, numerous product categories and duty exemption schemes disappeared, which has negatively impacted the exports of MSMEs.
- The agreement regarding products and their production techniques could potentially disadvantage Indian goods exports related to agriculture, foodgrains, and medicines, which may affect export volumes.
- The WTO consistency of income tax exemption has been a frequent topic of discussion within the WTO Trade Policy Review Mechanism forum. The income tax waiver on export earnings was executed as a temporary measure during the study period, and later in the trade policy 2009-14, India scrapped it. This severely disadvantaged Indian exports in the world market and caused severe fluctuations in the exports of goods.

- The Trade-Related Intellectual Property Rights (TRIPs) agreements mandate a stricter intellectual property rights framework. Bringing an amendment to the current legislation appropriately could affect a variety of MSME sectors that rely on technology sources for reverse engineering or are involved in counterfeit operations or using patented designs or trademarks. Only selected businesses or undertakings having their R&D will be able to take advantage of these changes. The software industry, which falls under copyright regulations, will benefit from this.
- Other quantitative limitations imposed by developed nations, which were to be abolished by 2015, will further open up greater trade possibilities for Indian textiles and garment exporters while also leading to increased competition in the global market.
- India is not equipped to manufacture a macro range of products; additionally, under a free trade policy (FTP) 2015-20, a complex system of customs and tariffs is projected to make local producers vulnerable when opened to FTAs, increasing imports and resulting in high trade deficits and inflation. The policy educates MSMEs on duty benefits under FTAs, indicating inefficient FTA use.
- The current FTP is subsidy-driven, with little focus on skill development and technological upgradation. Further, governmental subsidy schemes and policies towards MSME exporters notice specific sectors only. Government incentive schemes overlook several sectors, which can create several jobs and earn well from exports.
- The complaint claimed that the tax breaks provided to exporters under the SEIS and MEIS amounted to illegal export subsidies violating World Trade Organization rules. An incentive scheme for exporters to receive a certain percentage of duty credit scrips of the value of goods exported is included in the FTP 2015-20. Since India's per capita GDP is more than Rs. 81,349 annually, it has been removed from the category of "developing countries" that allow such incentives.

- The World Trade Organization Agreement on Technical Barriers to Trade (TBT) encourages the adoption of global standards. As an outcome of standardization, the domestic industry is expected to encounter tougher product quality standards in developed markets. However, manufacturers exporting those products that meet the Bureau of Indian Standards (BIS) may gain advantages from the agreement on technical trade barriers.

Due to the lowering of tariffs, elimination of quantitative restrictions, and various other initiatives following economic reforms, the degree of production available to the SME sector has significantly narrowed down. The domestic markets are becoming more competitive, while it is increasingly tough to penetrate the global export market; therefore, the MSME sector must improve its competitiveness.

6.2.2. Internal Problems

The economic reforms in India have exposed the SMEs sector to competition, but at the same time they have created opportunities. However, the capacity to capitalize on all these opportunities relies on addressing numerous intrinsic shortcomings within the small-scale industry sector. Following are the many inherent weaknesses found in the small-scale industry sector.

- Obsolete Technology
- Uncompetitive Prices
- Poor Quality
- Costly Credit
- Infrastructure such as power, roads, and communication should have backup systems in place.
- Plethora of labour legislation
- Lack of cohesion among micro, small, and medium-sized enterprises
- Ineffective associations
- Lack of information
- Logistics costs
- Costly product standards and certification procedures
- A restricted global experience and awareness of the consequences of the WTO agreements

- The absence of or limited alignment with global norms

We will now discuss the key elements that affect an enterprise's export activities and outcomes. The problems impacting the export performance of the small-scale industry sector are described below:

6.2.2.1. Technological Constraints

Technology is critical to product productivity, quality, competitiveness, and market acceptability. The technology employed by micro, small, and medium-sized enterprises in India is of low to moderate quality. The product quality in the MSME sector differs from that of foreign countries. R&D, which is very critical for making high-technology products, has not been the main focus of Indian SSIs. In high-technology industries, the competitive advantage is largely influenced by product innovation, which is often overlooked in the Indian MSME sector due to a lack of investment in R&D activities. In these products, the life cycle tends to be short, making it difficult to achieve a competitive edge due to certain constraints. As a result, MSMEs are generally not positioned to achieve a competitive advantage through their technical initiatives in high technology-based product lines.

6.2.2.2. Inadequate Finance and Credit

The lack of financial resources and credit is another barrier affecting exports from the small-scale industry sector. Better control of financial flow is crucial for any business, and accessibility of credit is vital for the effective operations of any industry. Inadequate and delayed credit remains the primary challenge confronting MSMEs.

"The problem is more acute in the case of micro-enterprises. Small enterprises lack access to the capital market. Investors are unwilling to invest in unquoted companies. Small businesses are perceived to be riskier in many developing countries; as a result, the cost of credit to small enterprises is high. It is not possible to have a credit rating for MSME units because of the cost involved in establishing the project viability compared to big enterprises. Assessing risk and monitoring small businesses involve higher costs. Returns are uncertain in the case of newly emerging hi-tech areas or new technologies."

Despite the various challenges, some potential solutions exist to address the eligibility criteria for financing in the MSME sector. The most concerning fact, however, is that only 16% of MSMEs have timely access to finance, forcing small and medium-sized businesses to rely on their own resources. This is a significant impediment to both companies and the MSME sector. This issue affects more than just small businesses. Larger firms also benefit because even the most prominent players require assistance in obtaining cheaper credit from traditional banks.

6.2.2.3. Infrastructure Bottlenecks

It is generally accepted that India's export capabilities are significantly underutilized because of infrastructure issues and their availability, such as power deficits, inadequate handling facilities, and transportation delays caused by poor communications across the country. The available infrastructure is not only insufficient, but the effectiveness and quality of its delivery are also quite inconsistent. The government's capacity to address these challenges in the coming years will also impact the supply aspect of Indian exports.

The lack of adequate infrastructure, especially in terms of electricity supply, communication networks, and telecommunication services, impacts production, costs, and delivery timelines. Frequent disruptions in the power supply negatively impact productivity, especially in advanced technology outputs. The demand for continuous power supply highlights small businesses' growing recognition of the importance of sustaining their quality and competitive advantage.

Similarly, enhanced and adequate telecommunication capabilities are required for MSME units operating in the fast-paced and technologically advanced international market. The demand for superior telecommunication services signifies a rising awareness among small firms regarding their importance. Executing hi-tech solutions to create and maintain better market relationships will also contribute to reducing the expenses associated with becoming a global player.

6.2.2.4. Size Constraints

The scale of business units determines the resources available to enterprises, which are essential for entering the global marketplace because of the advantages of economies of scale in both production and product marketing. As per studies, over 97 percent of MSME units are classified as small or micro-enterprises, traditionally utilizing outdated technology, which detrimentally impacts overall plant productivity, quality, and competitiveness of their products in the market. Consequently, this hampers their ability to export. Exporting might exceed the capabilities of very small units. Similarly, other MSMEs that benefit from protected domestic markets due to exclusive product manufacturing reservations or preferential government agreements may not venture into the global export markets.

6.2.2.5. Failure to Undertake Promotional Efforts

Businesses that engage in advertising and promotional activities tend to perform better than others in the global markets because they deliberately cultivate brand identities and trade names, as well as ensure product quality and customer satisfaction through post-sales support. Most MSMEs, facing challenges in resource availability to compete with large multinational enterprises in the global scenario, choose to sell their products to trading agencies or merchant exporters to sidestep direct competition. Similarly, it is challenging for them to create their own marketing channels in foreign markets or to forge normal relationships with branding and marketing firms that could help promote exports.

6.2.2.6. Managerial Capabilities

A large number of micro and small enterprises operate as single-person, family-run businesses and tend to centralize decision-making in just one or two individuals. For such businesses, the choice to enter export markets necessitates changes in management, sales and marketing strategies, production processes, and financial planning. Due to their limited managerial and technical skills, managing and controlling all the challenges associated with exports becomes a major hurdle. As a result, the controlling authority of an MSME must address these challenges before tackling the broader external challenges that arise when exploring export opportunities.

6.2.2.7. Marketing Constraints

From the beginning, marketing for SME products has remained a major challenge. The absence of proper and adequate marketing resources is a barrier that obstructs the exports of micro, small, and medium-sized enterprises. Those enterprises having formal connections and understanding with marketing companies in other countries have managed to maintain their exports. These organizations have an advantage in those markets as they have access to the latest information provided by various marketing networks of their foreign partners.

- Competition: Larger firms have forced MSMEs out of their marketplaces due to various factors, such as the rise of eCommerce and the advent of globalization. However, this phenomenon has been around for a while because MSMEs have faced competition since their inception, but they have dealt with it more successfully than professional firms. MSMEs continue to face competition in various industries, including agricultural machinery, clothing, and tourism.
- Skills: Regarding skills, Indian MSMEs lag far behind their counterparts in other countries because they rely heavily on underpaid informal workers and lack technical skills that can help boost productivity. As a result, smaller businesses are forced to take on jobs requiring low skill levels and expertise, which affects their long-term growth prospects.
- Lack of Professionalism: Despite being critical to the growth of larger industries, most Indian MSMEs lack professionalism. As a result, they are highly susceptible to corruption and abuse of power, which significantly impact their productivity.

The key challenges that the small-scale industries sector is encountering in different industry segments in exporting their products and which need proper attention are mentioned below:

- Transportation of goods from these firms by road or the rail network is highly expensive and time-consuming, which hinders the fulfilment of urgent export orders. There is a lack of railway wagons for partial loading, which impacts the transport of export cargo to seaports and the delivery of raw materials to manufacturing locations.

- The average turnaround time for a ship at the loading/unloading dock is usually no more than seven days, which somehow impacts and delays the shipment of goods at short notice. Shipping restrictions imposed by the port authorities on the loading and packing of synthetic enamel paints and primers, despite not being classified as cargo, affect export activities.
- The number of indirect taxes and very complicated documentation requirements place exporters at a significant disadvantage.
- The cost associated with export financing in India is higher compared to other nations.
- The cost of manufacturing becomes high and the competitiveness of products and processes is lost when labour is left unutilized during specific seasons, and the industry faces restrictions in laying off on- and off-roll workers due to labour law constraints.
- Organization-wise duty drawback rates are determined without considering the actual duty burdens reported by exporters in some cases, which leads to losses for exporters.
- The interest rate applied for any shortfall in meeting export obligations or other requirements is too high, which directly impacts cost competitiveness.
- Exports to other foreign nations in Indian rupees do not receive all the export advantages allowed for exports made against free foreign exchange.
- Various exporters encounter challenges in procuring export licenses in time for high-grade iron ore fines.
- Delays in procuring natural rubber via STC under the advanced licensing scheme impact the exportation of rubber products.
- The elevated cost of petroleum fuel typically increases the manufacturing expenses of glass and ceramic products, making them less competitive.

- Outdated equipment in the textiles and garments sector impacts quality, efficiency, and export levels.
- The computer application software exports of on-site services in the USA face various challenges due to visa limitations. Meanwhile, other countries are impeded by the lack of computer professionals skilled in regional languages.
- The software exports of off-site services face challenges because of dependence on satellite channels, which are hindered by unstable terrestrial telecommunication connections and high costs.

6.3. Exports Prospects

The launch of economic reforms and the establishment of the WTO have brought the MSME sector into different competitions; at the same time, they have presented various opportunities through increased access to the global market, encouragement for quality, productivity, and improved technology, along with the availability of raw materials and the required components. However, the advantage of globalization can only be fully realized if the issues related to exports are addressed and protective measures are implemented to utilize the available opportunities.

The MSME sector presents numerous opportunities because of the following factors:

- Requires less capital-intensive investment
- Extensive government advancement and support
- Small-scale business booking for exclusive product manufacturing
- Project profiles
- Funding, financing, and subsidies
- Machine procurement, raw material (RM) procurement, human resources training, and skills in both technical and managerial areas
- Support for manufacturing, tooling, and testing, reservation for exclusive Government procurement, and encouragement of export activities
- Increase in demand within the local market driven by overall economic growth

- Availability of labour at reasonable costs.

There are many areas where India has a comparative advantage and can establish a presence in the global market. The MSME sector in India now manufactures a diverse range of products, ranging from simple traditional consumer goods to highly advanced consumer goods. These sectors include Engineering goods, Chemicals and related products, Processed foods, Ready-made Garments, Electrical, Electronic and Computer application software, Finished Leather and Leather Products, Woollen Garments, Knitwear, Processed Tobacco and Snuff and Bidi, Spices, and a variety of others.

However, the potential for exporting from the MSME sector will rely on several factors. Some of the key components are highlighted below.

<u>6.3.1. Technology Upgradation and Modernization:</u>

Technological improvement and upgradation are essential for thriving in today's era of globalization and liberalization. It is nowadays critical for industrial advancement. The experience of advanced countries has clearly demonstrated that technological advancement and availability play an important role in rapid economic growth and social development.

One of the major challenges faced by MSMEs is technological obsolescence, including the use of outdated machinery and equipment. Technological upgradation and advancement have now become a necessity for these sectors. Thus, to remain competitive, the MSME sector must upgrade its obsolete technology and adopt new technologies, which may require modifications in the manufacturing process, the introduction of innovative tools and techniques for production, and the application of contemporary management and information technology. The Government of India should extend monetary assistance to MSME units for the purpose of technology and tools modernization.

The involvement of the Government in this area is appreciable. It provides support to MSME units through various organizations at the central, state, and district levels. The SIDO is a key player in technological advancement. To help the MSME sector, the Government offers resources such as tool rooms, product and development centres, testing centres, and central footwear training centres (CFTCs). Tool Rooms (TRs) have been set up to assist MSME industry units in improving technology by offering high-quality tooling resources, various training and consulting services, and standard service capabilities in the design and production of tools, fixtures, and moulds. Additionally, they provide extensive training in process and product development as well as machining, fitting of devices, and die-making.

The PPDCs have been established to focus on the specific challenges faced by industries, to develop and innovate new technologies, and to offer technical support services to MSME industries engaged in producing a variety of products, including export-worthy goods made available through the Local Testing Centres (LTCs). These centres conduct performance testing, type testing, acceptance testing, calibration services, and assist in developing different manufacturing processes. CFTCs provide support to MSME sectors by making manpower literate in the leather and footwear industry. The CFTCs situated in Agra and Chennai have been advanced with support from UNDP.

The SIDBI established a Technology Development and Modernization Fund (TDMF) scheme in April 1995 with a fund of Rs. 200 crores to provide direct help to MSME industries. The initiative's objectives are to encourage existing industrial units to upgrade their production and manufacturing facilities and adopt improved technology to enhance their export capabilities. The scheme offers support to cover expenses related to the purchase of capital equipment, acquisition of technical expertise, upgrading process technology and products, with a focus on improving quality in packaging and obtaining ISO 9000 series certification.

6.3.2. Promotion of Research and Development Activities

The marketing infrastructure for MSMEs comprises a mix of agencies and incentive programs. The NSIC registers MSMEs under a single-point registration system and secures orders for supplies from different suppliers. There are thirty-four subcontracting exchanges operating via the Small Industries Service Institutes (SISIs). These offices promote connections between large and medium-sized industries on the one hand and MSME ancillary units on the other, to secure subcontracting opportunities. These exchanges register MSMEs and identify which items can be outsourced from various public sector undertakings.

The lack of diversification in the export framework towards more technologically advanced products is attributed, in part, to the lower levels of R&D activities within Indian industries. R&D activity strengthens the global competitiveness of an enterprise through efficiency improvements and product innovation.

The MSME sector needs to be more focused and pay greater attention to diversification in this area. As a result, MSMEs must give more priority to research and development while concentrating on technologically advanced products to boost their export potential and hold a strong position in the global market. It is essential for the Government to evaluate, enhance, and unify the incentive framework for R&D activities in the country.

6.3.3. Improving Quality and Establishing Indigenous Brands

Quality improvement boosts global competitiveness since MSMEs primarily rely on outdated technology and old machinery, which impact the quality of their products. Therefore, the Government must focus on technological upgradation and modernization. It must create awareness of quality among MSME units to ensure they meet global standards. Also, it should create facilities to encourage the registration for global quality standards. The Government promotes the production of high-quality goods through National Quality Awards and incentives for ISO 9000 certification. However, more actions are needed, and the Government must enhance its efforts in this area.

Consumers abroad expect a high standard of quality, which should be upheld by MSME units. With proper implementation of marketing strategies, these units should consistently monitor and adapt to the evolving performance and demands of global consumers. Additionally, the significance of creating domestic brands through branding and advertising in global print and electronic media is essential for maintaining global competitiveness. Establishing a unique brand enables complete value upgradation. This sector, if focused on developing local brands, could benefit from monetary support for brand promotion activities and incentives for various products marketed under domestic brand names.

Promotion of Industrial Clusters: More than 60 percent of MSME exports come from industrial clusters. Hence, a significant initiative must be established to modernise these export-focused industrial clusters. MSMEs operating within clusters leverage their collective strength and gain advantages from both backward and forward economic linkages. Clusters promote specialisation in manufacturing, develop inter-firm relationships in production, enable labour division, and facilitate information exchange. These types of environments result in ongoing productivity and efficiency improvements and cultivate a network for sub-contracting between companies. Common resources such as technological upgradation, pilot projects, skill development, capacity building, efficient credit distribution, and promotional initiatives can be developed within industrial clusters. Clusters benefit from economies of scale and can enhance quality and reduce costs to meet global needs.

The country has experienced the spontaneous emergence of more than 1000 clusters, primarily without assistance from the state. This expansion has been driven by access to both domestic and global markets, along with low labour costs. However, the further advancement of these clusters faces significant obstacles due to outdated infrastructure, environmental degradation, technological obsolescence, and meagre workforce skills. Global experiences demonstrate that the growth of clusters can be supported through institutional development and enhanced by the provision of services and infrastructure development by the Government or non-government organisations.

SIDO has created technical support services via product-cum-process development centres to assist specific clusters of small-scale industry units for various specialised product lines.

- Removal of Procedural Hassles: Many laws, rules, and regulations are significant hurdles in the smooth progress of MSMEs in India. Various legislations, such as labour laws, the Factory Act, fiscal acts, municipal acts, and environmental acts, along with the inspectors who monitor MSME operations, often result in substantial harassment, delays, obstruction to work, and increased costs of production due to periodic payments. Until 2015, small industries were required to submit multiple returns, which hampered smooth workflow, as MSME units are typically managed by a single individual. However, this issue has been addressed with the initiation of a single-window tax payment system.

- Credit Facilities: The absence of finance and credit is a critical factor that hinders the growth of India's exports from the MSME sector. The on-time availability of adequate credit is essential for any economic unit, and the same applies to export-oriented MSME units. Credit must be both affordable and accessible. The Government of India has established several committees to assess the availability of credit for the MSME sector since the economic reforms of 1991. In the past two years, the Indian government has offered lower credit insurance premiums for exporters, faster disbursement of funds through the Export Credit Insurance Scheme, streamlined documentation requirements, and lower interest rates and premiums for small businesses. These assurances followed a 45 percent decrease in export credit disbursements by public sector banks in 2018-2019. Despite the promises, access to export credit in India remains limited. It is critical to promote financial assistance schemes among exporters actively. To raise awareness, the APEDA (Agricultural and Processed Food Products Export Development Authority) suggests that various export promotion councils hold workshops with exporters. Furthermore, the Trade Promotion Council of India indicates that financial institutions should take the following steps to improve credit:
    - Create a consolidated system to handle all applications, documentation, authorisations, approvals, and discrepancies. This would save exporters time and money when obtaining credit.
    - Create export credit products tailored to the needs of MSMEs.

- Simplification of Processes: India reduced the mandatory documents required for exports and imports in 2015. However, the paperwork burden remains high due to the requirement for additional copies. In its 2019 Economic Survey of India, the Organisation for Economic Co-operation and Development (OECD) suggested further reducing the number of export documents. It also called for reducing the time required for documentary and customs compliance. This recommendation is consistent with the Indian government's National Trade Facilitation Action Plan, which aims, among other things, to reduce cargo release time at ports for export shipments by 24 hours through initiatives such as:
  - Releasing shipments before customs duty has been finalised
  - Restricting new pre-shipment inspection requirements
  - Lowering the penalty for customs breaches that the trader voluntarily discloses
  - Reducing the number of documents and digitising their submission
- Cutting Tariffs: The consensus is that India's policy of levying high import tariffs to protect domestic industries is counterproductive. It not only makes local manufacturers less competitive but also harms the prospects of exporters who rely on imported inputs. According to the World Trade Organization's latest Trade Policy Review for India, tariffs should be reduced and made more straightforward and predictable. It claimed that frequent rate changes created uncertainty for traders. India's main trading partners, including the United States, have also requested tariff cuts. Players within the country have done the same. The Confederation of Indian Industry (CII) recommends a gradual transition to competitive tariffs over the next three years, with three tariff slabs proposed:
  - Zero percent to two percent for raw materials.
  - Two percent to five percent for intermediates.
  - Five percent to seven and a half percent for finished goods.

- Infrastructure Overhaul: In recent years, India has made progress in road construction. However, its maritime infrastructure still requires improvement. Here are some of the things India is doing and should be doing to improve its transportation infrastructure:
  - Modernise and Expand Ports: India launched "the Sagar Mala Programme" in 2015 with the goals of a) modernising existing ports, b) developing new ones, c) improving port connectivity, and d) ushering in port-linked industrialisation. The programme's 574 projects have a 2035 deadline. More ports are desperately needed in India. It has only one trans-shipment port, Kochi, and relies on Colombo, Singapore, and Port Klang in Malaysia for outbound goods trans-shipment. As a result, the proposal for a new trans-shipment hub in the Andaman and Nicobar Islands is very welcome.
  - Reduce Turnaround Time: It is critical to ease the export process by reducing the time it takes for cargo to enter and leave India's ports from the current 2.59 days. The government's plan to cut turnaround time to one to two days (the global average) by 2022-23 is a positive step.
  - Improve Road Connectivity: India is currently constructing 30 km of highway per day. This aligns with the goals of the Bharat Mala Programme, which aims to build new roads and create 9,000 km of economic corridors to improve connectivity between manufacturing centres, export hubs, and ports.
  - Indian Carrier Company: According to the Federation of Indian Export Organisations (FIEO), an indigenous shipping line would solve India's container and equipment shortages. The FIEO believes that a domestic carrier can control container rates, which have risen in the last year due to equipment shortages and port congestion.

6.4. The Barriers to Effective Implementation of Lean Production

Implementing lean production systems in India is proceeding slowly, even though the evidence is overwhelmingly in favor of its use to improve quality, increase productivity, and reduce delivery times. To clarify the significant implementation problems, I have investigated various secondary sources of information. The involved SMEs are within the manufacturing, electronics, clothing, glass, leather, FMCGs, and footwear industries.

Through analyzing the various secondary data obtained based on the interviews and questionnaires, the barriers to MSMEs' implementation of lean techniques have been identified in the following areas:

- Because of knowledge gaps, many industries have yet to hear of lean production: The application of lean manufacturing is uncommon. The primary reason is that lean production research and application are concentrated within universities, the Academy of Sciences, and a few large corporations. MSMEs in India are mainly focused on labor-intensive manufacturing industries. Laborers have a low level of knowledge, and few managers and skilled workers have higher education. Only a few managers in the investigated enterprises have heard of lean production.
- Misunderstanding of lean production: Through deep study, we find that there is a lot of misunderstanding in how lean production enterprises evolve:
  - ➢ Executing lean production requires a considerable investment and is primarily suitable for large organizations.
  - ➢ Lean production and manufacturing are applicable only to specific businesses and industries and are not relevant to our business organization.
  - ➢ Lean manufacturing began in Japan and is not suitable or applicable for our organization.
  - ➢ Lean manufacturing is a technique that we can learn and understand, provided we have adequate funds.
- Employees' resistance to lean manufacturing and production: Implementing lean manufacturing as a significant business

reform will encounter opposition from two sources. The initial factor arises from the organization's internal practices, including bad personal habits, feelings of insecurity, and moments of hesitation. For example, implementing 5S, the foundation for lean production, necessitates workers performing their daily tasks, keeping equipment maintained, maintaining a tidy workplace, and consistently enhancing individual skills. These actions will interfere with established personal routines, leading employees to experience feelings of insecurity and resentment.

Apart from the above, the traditional rights structure will be disrupted as a result of organizational changes, and some managers within the organization will obstruct the adoption of lean manufacturing or production.

- Mechanically implementing lean production without revising for the enterprise environment: The environment of Toyota, such as socioeconomic and cultural backgrounds, has gradually influenced the evolution of lean manufacturing. Based on the survey, there are a number of SMEs that execute lean production without fully comprehending what it entails, mistaking it for a specific technology. As a result, many lean production applications had the opposite effect of what was intended.
- The other challenges of implementing lean in India are –
  - ➢ Concentrated attention on individual tasks while the combined objectives for the development of the SME are ignored.
  - ➢ Even if the implementation is in process, the following problems lie ahead:
    - ✓ Use of methods without proper definition according to the characteristics of individual industries
    - ✓ Poor strategy for implementation
    - ✓ Shortage of essential resources needed for practice
- Lack of skills and training among the workers for proper implementation

- During project execution, the middle and top management do not provide proper support
- Improper understanding of the purposes and concepts of practicing lean
- Another challenge faced in MSMEs is cultural differences
- The rewards obtained from the implementation of lean are lacking
- There is limited consultation available for lean practice in MSMEs

6.5. Countermeasures to Implementing Lean Manufacturing Techniques for MSMEs

Implementing lean production means involves bringing in innovative management methods and techniques as well as completely new concepts and systems of management.

- The engagement and participation of top management: Introducing lean manufacturing in MSMEs, as a significant business transformation, is likely to encounter resistance from two sources. On the one hand, there is resistance from individuals within the organizations, which may stem from certain poor personal habits, personal insecurity, and illogical thinking. On the other hand, there is some organizational resistance. The principles of lean manufacturing focus on teamwork, people engagement, and the pull production technique, which contrast with the traditional approaches to management system thinking and methodologies.

Organizations that fail are frequently undervalued when it comes to their reluctance to undergo reform. To eliminate this resistance, top management must possess a wide understanding of management transformations and actively advocate for the reform process. Consequently, it is necessary to set up a skilled leadership team that holds credibility, has good decision-making authority, information, knowledge expertise, and strong interpersonal relationships to facilitate an effective transition.

According to the research work conducted by Henry Johnson, an American management science expert, approximately 43% of those surveyed believe that having a strong leadership team is an important factor contributing to successful reforms in business and management (Zhang & Yang, 2006).

- Good Communication Platform: An effective communication platform involves both "external" and "internal" platforms.

One reason lean manufacturing practices have not been widely accepted by MSMEs is that, in comparison to large organizations, they frequently do not have the resources or the skills necessary to uplift and develop their production systems (V. Axelson J., 2007). Another explanation is the "knowledge paradox," which occurs when an enterprise does not have sufficient information about lean manufacturing practices and the various improvement methods. One way to address this issue has been to establish networks with other enterprises to gain insights and implement lean principles and practices. Bititchi et al. emphasize the value of participants seeing value enhancement, whether it is internal or external (such as financial gain or personal satisfaction), in collaborative networks. This highlights the necessity for performance assessment on the web (Bititchi & Martinez, 2004).

On the other side, implementing lean manufacturing practices necessitates a robust internal communication system. Lean manufacturing demands active involvement from all organizational staff in the reform process, ensuring that their thoughts and actions are aligned. But this is a continuous long-term process.

Communication is the most important and the sole method in this process. In addition to this, training and learning serve as the most important means of communication.

Implementing lean production requires extensive training, which includes educating personnel on advanced management concepts (such as lean production and complete self-management) as well as highly advanced management and ground-test tools (such as 5S, Kanban, rationalization proposals, etc.).

Employees with different levels of knowledge will use standardized terminologies in day-to-day learning and interaction.

- Learning Organization: Inside and outside of the country, many managers realize that lean manufacturing is a set of tools and systems helping to manage operations better, yet it presents a complex initiative that Toyota has developed through long-term organizational learning and continuous improvement.

It is quite impossible for a macro-level transformation, such as executing lean manufacturing techniques, to be achieved overnight. The complete project rollout needs to be carefully planned, the managing team must develop a detailed understanding, and top management must support them in the plan without losing employee trust or motivation.

In the Toyota Production System (TPS), each employee is good at learning and engages in proactive thinking about continuous improvement, which holds great importance beyond merely learning. Being good at learning and acquiring skills is an important feature of the learning organization. In addition to that, improvements can be obtained when teams think and approach effectively in the improvement process.

A learning organization focuses on lifelong learning, the whole learning process, total learning, and group learning. In such an organization, it is essential for all individuals to participate in recognizing and solving issues, enabling the organization to constantly improve and enhance its capabilities.

Therefore, the country should develop learning-oriented organizations to adopt and execute lean manufacturing practices. With the availability of such capabilities, lean management strategies can be effectively applied, enabling organizations to gain and sustain their competitive edge.

- The Creation of a Performance Evaluation System: Bringing into place a lean management technique and developing a lean culture that shows tangible outcomes requires time. Measuring progress is critical in inspiring changes and improvement.

Short-term goals must be clearly defined and accurate to assess the targets we have taken, ensuring that manpower remains motivated to carry out reforms and that these reforms are not disrupted. The execution and visibility of results is not a short-term quick fix, but a long-term marathon journey. It sometimes takes days, months, or years to determine the outcomes of lean implementation. The disparity between the expected and actual outcomes may lead to a poor evaluation of lean performance. As a result, it is crucial to determine the progress made in lean implementations, such as product quality upgradation, operational cost reduction, increasing market share value, and improving customer satisfaction. These immediate successes will sustain employee enthusiasm and a sense of urgency.

In both Japanese and American manufacturing units, managers or workers often select performance metrics, like the defect rate, to track whether each worker meets their targets. However, it is important to recognize that performance evaluation needs to be well explained. This target includes two levels of meaning. First, the assessment should pertain to each member. Second, the evaluation should address specific business aspects, such as time and costs, as well as product quality.

6.6. Conclusion

The MSMEs sector faces both internal and external problems in exporting its products. Technological constraints, inadequate finance, credit, infrastructural bottlenecks, inability to undertake promotional activities, and size constraints, etc., are some essential internal factors adversely affecting exports. The external problems arising from reduced protection due to the removal of quantitative restrictions, lowering of tariffs, and other WTO-related measures pose many challenges before the MSMEs sector. This has increased competition both internally and internationally.

An adequate supply of credit, technological assistance, infrastructure, and low transaction costs are important for promoting small and medium-sized industries. This can be accomplished by establishing various links between businesses and their support institutions, forming partnerships between the private sector and the government, increasing the flow of critical information, and streamlining the legal and institutional framework.

The other problems MSMEs face are inappropriate managerial skills and production techniques, which hinder the increasing share of MSMEs in India's total exports. Another concern is the improper selection of operational tools for production. Firstly, there is a lack of understanding of lean production, staff resistance to change management, and instances where lean production is implemented mechanically without adjustments based on the business environment. Secondly, the implementation of lean manufacturing and production represents a revolutionary reform in the processes and work practices of all SMEs. For successful adoption of lean tools, MSMEs should engage in various productive measures that involve the commitment of top management, the establishment of effective communication, skilful and user-friendly learning platforms, and the setup of a system for rewards and recognition.

The prospects of exports from the MSMEs sector in India will purely depend on addressing the challenges associated with technological upgradation, credit facilities, infrastructure bottlenecks, marketing, quality improvement, cultural change, and appropriate managerial and operational tools for production, etc. The effort should be to take advantage of the opportunities created by the WTO and globalization. The guiding principle for the future course of MSMEs industry development should be accelerated growth and competitiveness. Therefore, MSMEs should improve the quality of their products and competitiveness.

Chapter 7| Conclusion and Findings

7.1. Summary

The MSME industry plays a crucial role in developing the Indian economy. Its contribution to GDP was nearly a third of the country's gross value added (GVA), while the MSME sector contributed almost half of its exports. Moreover, the industry is a significant employer, especially in the country's semi-developed and less-developed areas, helping reduce regional imbalances. The MSME sector also supports other industries by supplying raw materials and ancillary goods. However, the sector faces challenges in obtaining raw materials and the necessary funding. The government recognizes the importance of the sector and thus supports it through various financial incentives and training. These factors increase industry competitiveness while also boosting India's economic growth.

The research indicates that the MSME sector has achieved significant growth in broader aspects such as the number of units, level of production, opportunities for employment, and export activities. The outcomes of these sectors have shown a consistent rise between 2005-06 and 2019-20. It increased to Rs. 504665.81 crores in 2019-20, up from Rs. 120459.84 crores in 2005-06, reflecting a CAGR of 11.50 percent. The number of MSME units increased from 1.98 crores in 2005-06 to 4.25 crores in 2019-20, while employment within the sector rose from 4.08 crores in 2005-06 to 10.60 crores by 2019-20.

The analysis of the overall export performance suggests that MSMEs' exports rose at a CAGR of 11.50 percent per annum between 2005-06 and 2019-20. In comparison, India's total exports experienced a CAGR of 11.24 percent yearly during the study period. As a result, the percentage share of exports from MSMEs in traditional products increased from 51.35 percent in 2005-06 to 65.56 percent in 2019-20. This also holds true when we compare the yearly average growth rate of MSME sector exports with India's total exports from 2005-06 to 2019-20. The overall exports increased at a yearly average growth rate of 11.59 percent, while national product exports observed a minor decline to 9.98 percent. At the same time, exports from the MSME sector increased by 11.24 percent during the study period.

Thus, the rate of growth for total exports throughout the study duration was slightly higher than that of exports from the MSME sector. However, an important aspect of MSME units is that their proportion of overall exports has remained unchanged.

The proportion of individual items in total MSME sector exports varied widely during the study timeframe. In the conventional product category, the proportion of cashew kernels, liquid cashew nutshell, and spices fluctuated considerably, and their share declined in 2019-20 compared to the initial year 2005-06. However, the share of lac increased from 0.15 percent in 2005-06 to 1.12 percent in 2019-20. Within the non-traditional product group, for example, the share of electronic goods increased from 9.99 percent in 2005-06 to 16.01 in 2019-20. The proportion of chemicals and related products, plastic, finished leather and leather goods, processed food, and electronic and computer software increased by 0.95, 1.81, 6.63, 8.1, and 2.39 percent, respectively, in 2005-06 to 16.01, 4.69, 3.27, 8.07, 11.59, and 13.08 in 2019-20. The proportion of basic chemicals and medicines declined from 11.34 percent in 2005-06 to 11.17 percent in 2019-20. The share of marine products, woollen garments, sports goods, ready-made garments, rayon & synthetic products, and processed tobacco significantly declined. However, their share fluctuated widely during the period.

Though at the aggregate level, MSME sector exports performed well compared to the total exports of various goods and services from India, the calculation of major commodity exports from the MSME sector vis-à-vis total exports has yet to perform well even after decades of industrial revolutions. These challenges faced by the MSME sector led to this situation. The main challenges regarding MSME exports are as follows:

- Use of minimal technology
- Insufficient credit facilities
- Infrastructural bottlenecks
- Insufficient promotional efforts
- Inadequate marketing strategies
- Managerial constraints
- Constraints related to firm size

- Issues related to the WTO

However, it is not entirely correct to say that the MSME sector only suffers from weaknesses; it also possesses significant strengths. It is capable of tackling the challenges created in the new economic framework. Unlike large organizations, MSME industrial units feature a hierarchical management structure and distinct ownership, allowing them to be inherently adaptable and able to react quickly to market signals and shifts in consumer preferences. This makes MSMEs more innovative and receptive to new and unique ideas. MSME industrial units have lower manpower costs, which enable them to reduce the cost of production. In addition, these units are more engaged with their clients or customers, allowing them to stay attuned to evolving tastes and preferences.

7.2. SWOT Analysis

The study can also be understood and concluded through the deep explanation of SWOT (S-Strength, W-Weaknesses, O-Opportunities, T-Threats):

7.2.1. Strength

Based on different research work, it has been seen that the managing committee of MSME units offers flexibility and convenience in doing business. This makes effective cost control and efficient handling of operational challenges possible. Specifically, owners must maintain a close connection to the market and be adaptable to quickly respond to shifting market demands, which develops business strength. The potential for growth within the MSME sector is huge due to several contributing factors below:

- Adopting to Change: The micro and small enterprises are not involved much in the administrative process, so it is easy to adopt change.
- Good Customer Relation: The micro and small unit owners have a close relationship with their customers and clients, which leads to a sense of responsibility and maturity. They usually offer a more personalized approach to engage with

clients. Customers are regarded as family, which, of course, contributes to the growth and development of firms.

- Independence: Independence is another advantage of owning and operating a small business. One of the research studies on MSME enterprise units revealed that nearly 38% left their previous jobs to become their own bosses and market their own choices. In addition to this, many people aspire to make their own decisions, take risks, and enjoy the benefits of their hard work.
- Innovation and Creations: The micro units have the ability to develop and introduce new products and services more rapidly and creatively than large organizations bogged down by bureaucratic processes. Whether reacting to shifts in fashion, demographic changes, or advertising, a small business can typically reach decisions quickly rather than taking a month or so to decide.
- Address Customer Requirements: The MSME has the capability to modify its offerings to align with customer requirements. On average, these units have a deeper understanding of their customers compared to the typical employee in a big organization. If there is a change in the products or services offered, or even the hours of operation, which would improve customer satisfaction, a small business can execute those changes. Customers can also play a role in product and process development.
- Gestation Period: Mostly, the MSME has a shorter gestation period, indicating the time it takes for return on investment to the customer. Typically, this timeframe ranges from 2 to 5 years.
- Participation of People: Another benefit is that entrepreneurs, partners, employees, or even family members are inspired to achieve success. This encourages them to put in more effort and work more efficiently.

7.2.2. Weakness

From the perspective of shortcomings, the research work indicated that there is an absence of awareness regarding quality, support, and the proper selection of operational tools to produce goods at the lowest operating cost and with minimal waste. The highest weaknesses MSMEs face are a lack of technically advanced workers, lack of upgraded technology, lack of long-term strategic vision, and lack of infrastructure availability, which lead to obstacles in growth.

7.2.3. Opportunities

The current opportunities offer various benefits to MSMEs, including government assistance, protection for specific products, excise tax burden relief, and help for big organizations. Despite the prevailing weaknesses, MSMEs can seize opportunities presented by numerous bilateral and multilateral trade agreements, which provide a significant revenue stream for business owners and entrepreneurs. In the same way, enhanced credit support, along with various government initiatives to promote MSMEs, is being provided. Therefore, entrepreneurs and business owners can anticipate some easing in access to credit options. Additionally, the advent of the digital age has made access to new opportunities much easier and has expanded significantly. Several entrepreneurs have taken a stand against monopolies and have left their imprint on the industry. As a result, the rise of online marketplaces and alternative financing options has simplified the process for entrepreneurs to secure business funding. In addition to that, the National Small Industries Corporation (NSIC) has initiated numerous marketing and advertising programs to support these units. As a result, small business owners can access substantial marketing assistance from government entities to uplift the growth and development of MSMEs.

7.2.4. Threats

The challenges identified in this research include limited monetary resources, rivalry from large and global organizations, the risk of becoming technologically outdated, insufficient attention to various industrial training programmes, and rising costs of inputs. Therefore, the hindrances related to financial support should be somewhat excluded in the existing context. In the same way, as MSMEs face a volatile global economy and various significant challenges, SMEs might feel inclined to resort to bribery to secure their immediate survival. The recent increases in expenses such as salary costs, land, raw materials, and currency exchange, along with cash flow difficulties linked to collecting account receivables, have resulted in a highly difficult business landscape for MSMEs. Similarly, MSMEs encounter challenges in handling legal, regulatory, and cultural barriers, differences in different markets, and the difficulties involved in remote business management. These are the key areas that require concentration to overcome the threats and make progress.

7.3. Conclusion and Recommendations

MSMEs must upgrade the quality of their products and services to align with the global standard. The product must adhere to global standards to secure a strong position in the global market. Additionally, they must develop strategic planning practices that focus on the broader picture. A plan frequently highlights inconsistencies that need to be addressed, such as insufficient capital or other resources essential for supporting anticipated growth. Lean management techniques provide a means to pinpoint areas of weakness and create a plan to address those challenges. This can be accomplished without demanding a considerable amount of time, effort, or financial investment. Insufficient infrastructure also encompasses inadequate water supply, transportation, and other similar factors. MSMEs require assistance to set up their own independent power supply systems, as they are dependent on inconsistent energy provision from utility companies. An inadequate transportation management system (TMS) increases production costs. Hence, boosting credit support from the government, NGOs, and financial institutions is essential. Additionally, India has a large scale of human resources, but most labourers are unskilled. The big organizations are willing to offer good remuneration and invest significantly to onboard skilled employees. However, MSMEs often have to rely on unskilled or semi-skilled workers. Therefore, they require enhanced managerial skills. These challenges can be addressed through effective training and processes that empower them to become more competent in reaching their goals.

Likewise, when it comes to technology, only a limited number of firms operate with a sophisticated technology base, whereas most firms use old technology. They require quality and productivity improvements in their products. Because of their operations at a smaller scale, they are unable to benefit from economies of scale in production. In recent years, the Govt. has launched various technology upgrade programmes tailored for MSMEs. These initiatives have been launched by the Ministry of MSME. The objectives of these initiatives are to help small and medium-sized enterprises upgrade their technology and improve their production capabilities. Thus, the owners of MSMEs need to be informed about all the offers, schemes, and advantages available through the Govt. and other organizations for their advancement.

The MSMEs manufacture a diversified range of products, from very basic consumer products to advanced high-tech goods. This sector has the potential to excel in the international marketplace with certain products. These products include engineering goods, ready-to-use garments, basic chemicals, medicines and cosmetics, plastic items, processed foods, leather goods, electronic devices, marine products, etc. To reach a sustainable growth rate, the MSME sector needs to build and maintain competitiveness among the units required to face the challenges posed by globalization. Small and medium-sized enterprises (MSMEs) often find themselves caught up in daily management issues, leaving them with little time and resources to explore and adopt practices that could boost their productivity and competitiveness in the global market. The research study has revealed how lean management techniques have helped small and medium-sized industries become competitive and increase their contributions in the global market; we may also conclude here why implementing schemes for Lean Manufacturing is the need of the hour for MSMEs:

7.3.1. To Unleash Their Exponential Potential

Despite constituting more than 80% of the total number of industrial enterprises and supporting industrial development, many MSMEs in India face problems such as sub-optimal scale of operation, supply chain inefficiencies, technological obsolescence, and fund shortages. Owing to these challenges, the Government has set up guidelines for implementing the Lean Manufacturing Competitiveness Scheme under the National Manufacturing Competitiveness Program, which helps enhance MSMEs' manufacturing competitiveness by applying different Lean Manufacturing (LM) techniques.

7.3.2. To be Able to Compete with Global Players

Under the Lean Manufacturing Competitiveness Scheme, MSMEs are assisted in reducing their overall manufacturing costs through various Lean Tools such as: 5S System, Visual Management and Control, Standard Operating Procedures (SOPs), Just In Time (JIT), KANBAN System, Cellular Layout, Value Stream Mapping (VSM), Mistake Proofing, Single Minute Exchange of Die (SMED), Total Productive Maintenance (TPM), Rapid Improvement Process, etc. From proper personnel management and better space utilization to scientific inventory management and improved process flows – the various tools of workplace management help increase productivity, inculcate sound management systems, and foster a culture of continuous improvement.

7.3.3. To Benefit from the 80% Subsidy Offered by the Government of India

The Lean Manufacturing Competitiveness Scheme is implemented in clusters. With the help of financial assistance, a mini cluster gets a lean consultant for 18 months to implement specific Lean Manufacturing techniques. This support serves as a backbone to the MSME units. The Government bears a maximum of 80% of the project cost for each cluster, and the MSME pays the remaining 20%.

7.3.4. Enabled Huge Savings

Under the pilot phase, more than 1000 MSMEs have completed Lean Implementation and reported more than Rs. 100 Crores in annual savings. The other achievements were as follows:

- Increase in Productivity (Avg.) by ~ 50 - 80%
- Increase in production capacity by ~ 10 - 15%
- Increase in inventory turnover by ~ 20 - 25%
- Space reclaimed for productive work by ~ 10 - 20%
- Reduction in manufacturing lead time by ~ 10% - 30%
- Export potential gain by ~ 5% – 10%
- Number of improvements done: more than 10,000

- Hence, Lean will help an MSME improve its overall quality, eliminate waste, reduce total cost, and decrease the time it takes to finish an activity from start to finish. Through the deployment of Lean Tools, various qualitative, quantitative, and monetary benefits, along with expected contributions to exports, are likely to be achieved. The following measures can also expand the output and exports from the MSME sector:
- Technology upgradation and modernization
- Expansion of credit facilities
- Removal of infrastructural and production bottlenecks
- Wider exposure to marketing and promotional activities
- Promotion of research and development
- Improvement in product quality and brand building
- Promotion of agglomeration and industrial clusters
- Removal of procedural hassles

Thus, prospects for exports from the MSME sector will depend upon the competitiveness of this sector in the world market. The industry has to improve its efficiency to meet global requirements, ensure the quality of its products is up to international standards, and reduce the cost of production by enhancing productivity with lean techniques. It also has to adopt aggressive branding and marketing techniques to make a place in the world export market.

References

i. Achanga, P., Shehab, E., Roy, R., & Nelder, G. (2006). Critical success factors (CSF) for lean implementation within SMEs. *Journal of Manufacturing Technology Management, 17*(4), 460–471.

ii. Anand, G., Ward, P. T., & Tatikonda, M. V. (2009). Dynamic capabilities through continuous improvement (CI) infrastructure. *Journal of Operations Management, 27*(6), 444–461.

iii. Annual Report; Ministry of Micro, Small and Medium Enterprises, Government of India. https://www.india-briefing.com/news/micro-small-medium-enterprises-india-explainer-17887.html/

iv. Bhuiyan, N., & Baghel, A. (2005). An overview of continuous improvement (CI), from the past to the present. *Management Decision, 43*(5), 761–771.

v. DCMSME Report. Evaluating lean performance of Indian small and medium sized industries. http://www.dcmsme.gov.in/publications/comitterep/abid.htm

vi. Deming Institute, The W. Edwards. (2016). Theories of profound knowledge. https://www.deming.org/theman/theories/profoundknowledge

vii. Kimberly, D., Shweta, C., & Gretchen, A. M. (2017). Lean adoption in small and medium enterprise: Model variation. *The Journal of Technology, Management, and Applied Engineering, 33*(3).

viii. Majava, J., & Ojanpera, T. (2012). Lean production development in SMEs: A case study. *Management and Production Engineering Review, 8*(2), 41–48.

ix. Nikaido, Y. (2004). Technical efficiency of small-scale industry: Application of stochastic production frontier model. *Economic and Political Weekly, 39*(6), 592.

x. Prasad, C. S. (2004). *Small and medium enterprises in global perspective: Employment generation, Vision 2012*. New Century Publications.

xi. Rahman, N. A., Sharif, S., & Esa, M. (2013). Lean manufacturing case study along with Kanban system implementation. *Procedia Economics and Finance, 7,* 174–180.

xii. Rommelfanger, H. J., & Eickemeier, S. H. (2013). *Entscheidungstheorie: Klassische Konzepte und Fuzzy-Erweiterungen*. Springer-Verlag.

xiii. R. K. Tiwari, & J. K. Tiwari. (2018). Evaluating lean performances of Indian small and medium sized enterprises. *Open Engineering, 8,* 293–306. De Gruyter.

xiv. Thanki, S., Govindan, K., & Thakkar, J. (2016). An investigation on lean green implementation practices in Indian SMEs using analytical hierarchy process (AHP) approach. *Journal of Cleaner Production, 135,* 284–298.

xv. MSME Sector Contributes Significantly to Indian Economy. https://pib.gov.in/Pressreleaseshare.aspx?PRID=1579757

xvi. Yang, C. C., & Chen, B. S. (2004). Key quality performance evaluation using fuzzy AHP. *Journal of the Chinese Institute of Industrial Engineers, 21*(6), 543–550.

xvii. Yadav, O. P., Goel, P. S., Jain, R., & Mohanty, R. (2010). Insights and learnings from lean manufacturing implementation practices. *International Journal of Services and Operations Management, 6*(4), 398–422.

xviii. Yusup, M. Z., Mahmood, W. H. W., & Salleh, M. R. (2016). Implementation of lean practices based on Malaysian manufacturers' perspective: A confirmatory factor analysis. *International Journal of Advanced Operations Management, 8*(2), 105–139.

xix. Alias Sunita Kulkarni, B., & Mishrikoti, A. H. (2019). Lean practices in SMEs towards improvement in production performance: A research. *International Journal of Recent Technology and Engineering (IJRTE), 8*(2S3). https://doi.org/10.1234/ijrte

xx. Annual Report 2021-22. (2022). Ministry of Micro, Small & Medium Enterprises, Government of India.

xxi. Cooney, R. (2002). Is 'Lean' a universal production system? *International Journal of Operations & Production Management, 22,* 1130–1147.

xxii. Directions for Manufacturability. (n.d.). Manufacturability in India. https://manufacturabilityinindia.blogspot.com/

xxiii. e-Book on schemes for MSMEs. (n.d.). Ministry of Micro, Small and Medium Enterprises, Government of India.

xxiv. Kakinada Hope Island Development. (2019, August). *MENA Report,* Albawaba (London) Ltd.

xxv. Loan Apply, How to Apply MSME Loan Online. (n.d.). Money View. https://moneyview.in/loan-insights/how-to-apply-for-msme-loan

xxvi. Pal, S. (2023). Causes of excess capacity. *arXiv.* http://arxiv.org/abs/2304.02137

xxvii. SAP-LAP models of inquiry. (2000). *Management Decision, 38*(5), 347–353.

xxviii. [Lean Manufacturing Guidelines]. (n.d.). Ministry of Micro, Small & Medium Enterprises, Government of India. https://msme.gov.in/sites/default/files/guidelines%20lean.pdf

xxix. Lean Manufacturing. (n.d.). Ministry of Micro, Small & Medium Enterprises, Government of India. https://msme.gov.in/lean-manufacturing

xxx. [DCMSME]. (n.d.). Office of the Development Commissioner, Ministry of Micro, Small & Medium Enterprises. http://www.dcmsme.gov.in/JDC

xxxi. [Library Record]. (n.d.). Universitas Indonesia Library. https://lib.ui.ac.id/detail?id=20500049&lokasi=lokal

xxxii. Ghosh, M. (2012). Lean manufacturing (LM) performance in Indian manufacturing plants. *Journal of Manufacturing Technology Management (MTM), 24*(1), 113–122.

xxxiii. Guru Murthy, A., & Kodali, R. (2011). Design of lean manufacturing systems (LMS) using value stream mapping (VSM) with simulation: A case study. *Journal of Manufacturing Technology Management (JMTM), 22*(4), 444–473.

xxxiv. H.H. Ricondo Iriondò, I., Serrano Lasa, I., & De Castro Vila, R. (2016). Takt time as a lever to introduce lean production in mixed engineer-to-order/make-to-order machine tool manufacturing companies. *International Journal of Industrial Engineering, 23*(2).

xxxv. H.H. Tomas Rohac, & Jenuska, M. (2015). 25th At the DAAAM International Symposium on Intelligent Manufacturing and Automation. In *Procedia Engineering* (pp. 520–529).

xxxvi. Kumar, S. S., & Kumar, M. P. (2014). Cycle time reduction of a truck body assembly in the automobile industry by lean principles. *Procedia Materials Science, 5,* 1853–1862.

xxxvii. Marasini, B., Kharel, S., Deo, N. K., & Gupta, B. (2014). A model for LM in Indian MSME. *IJSETR, 3*(5).

xxxviii. Omack, J. P., & Jones, D. T. (1997). Lean thinking—Banish waste and create wealth in your corporation. *Journal of the Operational Research Society (JODRS), 48*(11), 1148–1148.

xxxix. Rommelfanger, H. J., & Eickemeier, S. H. (2013). *Entscheidungstheorie: Klassische Konzepte und Fuzzy-Erweiterungen.* Springer-Verlag.

xl. Sundar, R., Balaji, A. N., & Kumar, R. S. (2014). A review on the lean manufacturing implementation techniques. *Procedia Engineering, 97,* 1875–1885.

xli. Tsvetanov, P. E., & Mikhailov, L. (2004). Reasoning under uncertainty during pre-negotiations using fuzzy AHP.

xlii. Venkataraman, K., Ramnath, B. V., Kumar, V. M., & Elanchezhian, C. (2014). Application of value stream mapping (VSM) to reduce a machining process's cycle time (CT). *Procedia Materials Science, 6,* 1187–1196.

xliii. Vinod, S., & Joy, D. (2012). Structural equation modeling of lean manufacturing practices. *International Journal of Production Research (IJPR), 50*(6), 1598–1607.

xliv. Yang, C. C., & Chen, B. S. (2004). Key quality performance evaluation using fuzzy AHP. *Journal of the Chinese Institute of Industrial Engineers (CIIE), 21*(6), 543–550.

xlv. Yadav, O. P., Nepal, Goel, B. P. S., Jain, R., & Mohanty, R. P. (2010). Insights and learnings from lean manufacturing implementation practices. *IJSOM, 6*(4), 398–422.

xlvi. De Gruyter. (2018). https://www.degruyter.com/document/doi/10.1515/eng-2018-0032/html

xlvii. Almannai, B. (2008). A decision support tool based on QFD and FMEA for the selection of manufacturing automation technologies. *Science Direct, 24*(4), 501–707.

xlviii. Bottani, E. (2009). A fuzzy QFD approach to achieve agility. *Science Direct, 119*(2), 380–391.

xlix. Bottani, E., & Rizzi, A. (2006). Strategic management of logistic service: A fuzzy QFD approach. *Science Direct, 103*(2), 585–599.

l. Kumar, V., & Chaturvedi, S. K. (2011). Prioritization of maintenance tasks on industrial equipment for reliability: A fuzzy approach. *International Journal of Quality & Reliability Management (IJQRM), 28*(1).

li. Mandal, S., & Maiti, J. (2014). Risk analysis using FMEA: Fuzzy similarity value and possibility theory-based approach. *Science Direct, 41*(7), 3527–3537.

lii. Ookalkar, A. D. (2009). Quality improvement in haemodialysis process using FMEA. *International Journal of Quality & Reliability Management (IJQRM), 26*(8).

liii. Parameshwaran, R. (2018). Fuzzy integrated QFD, FMEA framework for the selection of lean tools in a manufacturing organization. *The Management of Operations, 29*(5), 403–417.

liv. Sawhney, R. (2010). A modified approach to enhance reliability of lean system. *International Journal of Quality & Reliability Management (IJQRM), 27*(7), 832–855.* https://doi.org/10.1108/02656711011062417

lv. Souza, B., & Carpinetti, R. (2014). A FMEA-based approach to prioritize waste reduction in lean implementation. *International Journal of Quality & Reliability Management (IJQRM), 31*(4).

lvi. Yager, R. (1981). A procedure for ordering fuzzy subsets of the unit interval. *Science Direct, 24*(2), 143–161.

lvii. Grin. (n.d.). Retrieved from

https://www.grin.com/document/518385

lviii. Academia.edu. (n.d.). Lean manufacturing quiz. Retrieved from https://www.academia.edu/39006694/LEAN_Manufacturing_Quiz

lix. Dr. Ghouse, S. M. (2014). Export competitiveness of India: The role of MSMEs to play. *International Journal of Management Research & Review, 11*(6), 1069–1084.

lx. Dr. Peter, P. (2018). Export performance of small-scale industries in India. *Indian Journal of Economics and Development, 6*(11), 1–8.

lxi. Patil, S., & Dhawan, R. R. (n.d.). Analysis on export performance: MSMEs in India. *Journal of Architecture & Technology.* Issue No. 1006-7930.

lxii. CII. (n.d.). Events details. https://cii.in/EventsDetails.aspx

lxiii. Financial Express. (2022). MSME exim share of MSMEs in India's total exports declined from nearly 50%: Govt data. https://www.financialexpress.com/industry/sme/msme-exim-share-of-msmes-in-indias-total-exports-declined-from-nearly-50-govt-data/2598711/

lxiv. HDFC Bank. (2022). Know evolution of India's MSME sector. https://www.hdfcbank.com/personal/resources/learning-centre/sme/know-evloution-of-indias-msme-sector-2022

lxv. IBEF. (n.d.). MSME industry. https://www.ibef.org/industry/msme

lxvi. Macrotrends. (n.d.). India exports. https://www.macrotrends.net/countries/IND/india/exports

lxvii. ORF. (n.d.). Exploring India's manufacturing exports dynamics. https://www.orfonline.org/expert-speak/exploring-indias-manufacturing-exports-ynamics/

lxviii. Trade Statistics. (n.d.). Export import database. https://tradestat.commerce.gov.in/eidb/default.asp

lxix. World Bank. (n.d.). WITS country profile: India. https://wits.worldbank.org/CountryProfile/en/Country/IND/Year/LTST/TradeFlow/Export/Partner/all/

lxx. Alam, A. (2005). Role of small-scale industries in India's export since 1991 (Doctoral thesis, Department of Economics, Aligarh Muslim University, Aligarh).

lxxi. Bititci, U., Martinez, V., Albores, P., & Parung, J. (2004). Creating and managing value in collaborative networks. *International Journal of Physical Distribution & Logistics Management, 34*(3/4), 251–268. https://doi.org/10.1108/09600030410545443

lxxii. Bhuvaneswari, A. S., & Mishrikoti, A. H. (2019). Lean practices in SMEs towards improvement in production performance: A research. *International Journal of Recent Technology and Engineering (IJRTE), 8*(2S3).

lxxiii. Cogoport. (n.d.). 4 problems exporters in India face and their solutions. https://www.cogoport.com/blogs/4-problems-exporters-in-india-face-and-their-solutions

lxxiv. Financial Express. (2021). MSME EXIM: MSMEs' longer wait for new foreign trade policy may stifle their growth. https://www.financialexpress.com/industry/sme/cafe-sme/msme-exim-msmes-longer-wait-for-new-foreign-trade-policy-may-stifle-their-growth/2360456/

lxxv. Kumar, N. (2004). India's trade in 2020: A mapping of relevant factors in India. In *India Vision 2020, the report plus background papers* (p. 873). Planning Commission, GOI; Academic Foundation.

lxxvi. Lendingkart. (n.d.). Major challenges faced by the MSME sector & their impacts. https://www.lendingkart.com/blog/major-challenges-faced-by-the-msme-sector-their-impacts/

lxxvii. Report of the Working Group on Micro, Small & Medium Enterprises (MSMEs) growth for 12th five-year plan (2012-17). (n.d.). https://msme.gov.in/report-working-group-msme-growth-12th-five-year-plan-2012-17

lxxviii. Von Axelson, J. (2007). On the development of production methods for transfer to small to medium-sized enterprises (Doctoral thesis, Department of Production Engineering, The Royal Institute of Technology).

lxxix. Yang, P., & Yu, Y. (2010). The barriers to SMEs' implementation of lean production and countermeasures. *International Journal of Innovation, Management and Technology, 1*(2).

lxxx. Zhang, J., & Yang, W. (2006). The obstacles in corporate organizational reform. *Business Studies, 9,* 78–81.

lxxxi. 4C Consulting. (n.d.). 5 reasons why MSMEs must consider lean manufacturing schemes. https://www.4cpl.com/blog/5-reasons-why-msmes-must-consider-lean-manufacturing-schemes/

lxxxii. Alias, B., Kulkarni, S. M., & Anand, H. M. (2019). Lean practices in SMEs towards improvement in production performance: A research. *International Journal of Recent Technology and Engineering (IJRTE), 8*(2S3).

lxxxiii. Economic Division. (2020, September). *Monthly economic review.* Department of Economic Affairs.

lxxxiv. Ministry of Micro, Small and Medium Enterprises, Government of India. (2018, November 1). Unlocking the potential of MSME exports: Strategy action plan. https://[link if available]

List of Tables

List of Figures

List of Acronyms

AHP	:	Analytic Hierarchy Process
APEDA	:	Agricultural and Processed Food Products Export Development Authority
BPM	:	Business Process Management
BIS	:	Bureau of Indian Standards
CAGR	:	Compound Annual Growth Rate
CFTC	:	Central Footwear Training Centers
CI	:	Continuous Improvement
CM	:	Cellular Manufacturing
CFT	:	Cross Functional Team
CAGR	:	Compound Annual Growth Rate
CSF	:	Critical Success Factor
CII	:	Confederation of Indian Industry
DCMSME	:	Development Commissioner of Micro Small and Medium Enterprises
DGCIS	:	Directorate General of Commercial Intelligence & Statistics
ENVA	:	Essential Non-Value Added
FFA	:	Factory Fundamental Activities
FAHP	:	Fuzzy Analytical Hierarchy Process
FMEA	:	Failure Modes and effects Analysis
FFMEA	:	Fuzzy Failure Modes and Effects Analysis
FQFD	:	Fuzzy Quality Function Deployment
FLRPN	:	Fuzzy Lean Risk Priority Number
FTP	:	Free Trade policy
FTA	:	Free Trade Agreement
GDP	:	Gross Domestic Product
GOI	:	Government Of India
GR	:	Growth Rate
GVA	:	Gross Value Added
HFA	:	Hub Fundamental Activities
IBEF	:	Indian Brand Equity Foundation
IT	:	Information Technology
ISO	:	International Organization for Standardization
ISM	:	Interpretive Structural Modeling
IRDA	:	Insurance Regulatory and Development Authority

IPR	:	Intellectual Property Rights
JIT	:	Just In Time
KPI	:	Key Performance Indicator
LM	:	Lean Manufacturing
LMC	:	Lean Manufacturing Consultant
LAP	:	Learning Action Performance
LFT	:	Lean Failure Tools
LFM	:	Lean Failure Mode
LP	:	Lean Production
MSME	:	Micro Small and Medium Enterprises
MIT	:	Massachusetts Institute of Technology
MEIS	:	Merchandise Exports from India Scheme
NPC	:	National Productivity Council
NA	:	Nonvalue Added
NTG	:	Non-Traditional Goods
NSIC	:	National Small Industries Corporation
OEE	:	Overall Equipment Effectiveness
OGL	:	Open General License
OEM	:	Original Equipment Manufacturer
OECD	:	Organization for Economic Cooperation and Development
PDCA	:	Plan Do Check Act
PPS	:	Pull Production System
PPC	:	Production Planning and Control
PM	:	Preventive Maintenance
PPM	:	Product and Production Method
QC	:	Quality Control
QCI	:	Quality Council of India
QFD	:	Quality Function Deployment
R&D	:	Research and Development
RBI	:	Reserve Bank of India
RM	:	Raw Material
SCM	:	Subsidies and Countervailing Measures
SEM	:	Structural Equation Modelling
SLR	:	Simple Linear Regression
SME	:	Small and Medium Enterprises
SMED	:	Single-Minute Exchange of Die
SIDBI	:	Small Industry Development Bank of India

SWOT	:	Strength Weakness Opportunities and Threats
SPV	:	Special Purpose Vehicles
SOP	:	Standard Operations Procedures
STS	:	Socio Technical System
SAP	:	Situation Actor Process
SIDO	:	Small Industry Development Organization
SISI	:	Small Industries Service Institutes
SEIS	:	Service Exports from India Scheme
TMS	:	Transport Management System
TPM	:	Total Productive Maintenance
TQC	:	Total Quality Control
TQM	:	Total Quality Management
TEE	:	Total Employee Engagement
TR	:	Tool Room
TBT	:	Technical Barriers to Trade
TG	:	Traditional Goods
TPRM	:	Trade Policy Review Mechanism
TRIPS	:	Trade Related Intellectual Property Rights
TDFM	:	Technology Development and Modernization Fund
UNDP	:	United Nations Development Programme
VSM	:	Value Stream Mapping
VA	:	Value Added
WTO	:	World Trade Organization
ZED	:	Zero Defect Zero Effect

Annexure

Evaluation: About the Firm

1	**Name of the firm**					
2	Age of the firm	**1**	**2**	**3**	**4**	**5**
		0-1 Year	1-5 Year	5-10 Year	10-15 Year	>15 Year
3	Form of the company	Proprietor	Partnership	Pvt. Ltd.		
4	Name of the owner					
5	Age of the owners	1	2	3	4	5
		<25	25-30 Year	30-40 Year	40-50 Year	>50 Year
6	Name of the Executive considered					
7	Designation					
8	Qualification - Technical	No Education	Fundamental	Non-Technical	Technical	Tech – Comme
9	Size of the firm	1	2	3	4	5
		Micro ≤1 Crore	Small 1 - 10 Crore	Medium 10 - 50 Cr.	Investment made except land and building only	
10	No of employees working	Admin	Production	Others		
11	Type of Industry (Nature of Manufacturing Process)	Job Order	Part Supplier	Product Manufacturer		
12	Quality Management - Certification	Yes	No			
13	Turn Over of the firm	<1 Cr	1 - 2 Cr	2 - 5 Cr	5 – 10 Cr	>10 Cr
14	Turn Over Details	Value	%			
A	Export Turn Over					
B	Local Turn Over					

C	Job Order					
D	Total					
15	List of Customer ant their QMS Certification details					
16	Lean or OMS Initiatives	Yes	No			
A	Lean Level	1	2	3	4	5

Objective 1: To Study the Level of Awareness about the Lean Management

Sr. No.	**List of Tools used in Lean Manufacturing**	**0 Not Known**	**1 Just Known**	**2 Average Knowledge**	**3 Good Knowledge**	**4 Excellent Knowledge**
1	5S (Workplace management)					
2	Andon (Visual feedback system)					
3	Bottle Neck Analysis					
4	Continuous Flow					
5	Gemba (The real place)					
6	Heijunka (Level Scheduling)					
7	Hoshin Kanri (Policy deployment)					
8	Jidoka (Automation)					
9	Just In Time (JIT)					
10	Kaizen (Continuous Improvement)					
11	Kanban (Pull System)					

12	KPI (Key Performance Indicator)					
13	Muda (West)					
14	OEE (Over All Equipment Efficiency)					
15	PDCA (Plan Do Check Act)					
16	Poka – Yoke (Mistake proofing)					
17	Root Cause Analysis					
18	SMED (Single Minutes Exchange of Die)					
19	Six Big Losses					
20	SMART Goals					
21	Standardized Work (SOP) Standard					
22	Takt Time (Production line balancing)					
23	TPM (Total Productive Maintenance)					
24	VSM (Value Stream Mapping)					
25	Visual Factory					

Objective 2: To Study the Level of Implementation of Lean Tools

Sr. No.	**List of Tools used in Lean Manufacturing**	**0 Not Initiated**	**1 Under Awareness**	**2 Just Introduced**	**3 Partially Implemented**	**4 Fully Implemented**
1	5S (Workplace management)					
2	Andon (Visual feedback system)					

3	Bottle Neck Analysis					
4	Continuous Flow					
5	Gemba (The real place)					
6	Heijunka (Level Scheduling)					
7	Hoshin Kanri (Policy deployment)					
8	Jidoka (Automation)					
9	Just In Time (JIT)					
10	Kaizen (Continuous Improvement)					
11	Kanban (Pull System)					
12	KPI (Key Performance Indicator)					
13	Muda (West)					
14	OEE (Over All Equipment Efficiency)					
15	PDCA (Plan Do Check Act)					
16	Poka – Yoke (Mistake proofing)					
17	Root Cause Analysis					
18	SMED (Single Minutes Exchange of Die)					
19	Six Big Losses					
20	SMART Goals					
21	Standardized Work (SOP) Standard					
22	Takt Time (Production					

	line balancing)					
23	TPM (Total Productive Maintenance)					
24	VSM (Value Stream Mapping)					
25	Visual Factory					

Objective: 3: To Identify the Hurdles in Implementing Lean Management Tools

Sr. No.	Details	0 Not at all	1 Very Less	2 Average	3 Very Much	4 Worst Hit
A	Resource Related Hurdles					
1	Financial Requirement					
2	Lean Management Subject Details					
3	Support of Software and Hardware					
4	Literature and course material availability					
5	Training facility, trainer availability					
B	Time Schedule Related					
1	Day to day work commitment					
2	Customer concentration					
3	New product development					
4	High market sensitivity (frequent variant change)					
5	Turn Over Targets (Rewards and recognitions)					
6	Others					
C	Policy Decisions					
1	Management Commitment (Change in Priority)					
2	Trade secret					

3	Lack of Internal communication					
4	Line and Staff Conflicts					
5	High skilled Employee Attrition					
6	Others					
D	Skills and Competence					
1	Right Person and Right Job					
2	Change Restriction					
3	Job Security					
4	Union and Labor Restriction					
5	Language					
6	Others					
E	External Environment					
1	Customer Support					
2	Market Inconsistency					
3	Government Policy					
4	Heavy Competition					
5	Technological Advancement					
6	Others					

Objective 4: To Assess the Effectiveness of the Lean Implementation

Sr. No.	**Improvements Area**	**1**	**2**	**3**	**4**	**5**
		0%	**Up to 5%**	**5-10%**	**10-15%**	**>15%**
1	Productivity					
2	Quality					
3	Cost					
4	Delivery					
5	Safety					

Objective 5: To Identify the Solotions to Overcome the Hurdles

Sr. No.	**Area**	**1**	**2**	**3**	**4**	**5**
		Not at All	**Very Less**	**Average**	**Very Much**	**Worst Hit**
1	Time					
2	Knowledge					
3	Customer Support					

4	Management Confident on the System					
5	Reliability on Employees					